How to Write a Précis

How to Write a Précis

PAMELA RUSSELL

School of Translators and Interpreters
Faculty of Arts
University of Ottawa

University of Ottawa Press

Canadian Cataloguing in Publication Data

Russell, Pamela R. (Pamela Ruth), 1947-
How to write a précis

ISBN 0-7766-0143-1

1. Abstracting.   2. Abstracting—Problems,
exercises, etc.   I. Title.

PE1477.R98 1988   808'.062   C88-090306-6

59,94ᴾ

UNIVERSITÉ   UNIVERSITY
D'OTTAWA   OF OTTAWA

Typesetting by Reprographic Services
University of Ottawa

Text and cover design by Peggy Heath

Table of Contents

PART TWO

Preface

How to Write a Précis should be of interest to language teachers and language students in general, and to teachers and students of translation in particular.

The material in this book was compiled primarily for use by students and teachers of translation at the university level. The précis is an exercise that is admirably suited to developing language skills, and the exercises presented here were initially developed and used in first-language and second-language courses for translation students.

But the applications of the précis extend far beyond translator training. Précis-writing has often been a component of high school courses in English composition, and the guidelines and exercises presented in this text would certainly be of interest to secondary school English teachers. Moreover, since the scope of this book goes well beyond the introductory approach found in secondary school textbooks, the material included herein could be applied to a wide variety of post-secondary courses in communication skills, writing techniques, and business English.

To the Teacher

Précis-writing is an excellent exercise for developing students' writing skills. This manual can be used to advantage by teachers of all types of English composition. The manual, accompanied by a good English grammar book, can provide the basis for a full writing course. In addition,

it can be easily used as a complement to other texts and material in an English language course, and instructors can select just those exercises which are appropriate for their classroom. The exercises and texts provided are of varying difficulty, and the teacher can choose those which suit the level of proficiency and the special interests of a particular group of students.

This book will also be of value to second-language teachers. Précis-writing can play a key role in second-language teaching; it develops both passive and active language skills by requiring the student to both read and write in his or her second language. In addition to being a vehicle for teaching second-language writing techniques, it also provides a framework for exposing the student to interesting texts written in a variety of styles and on a variety of topics in the second language.

To the Student

This book contains a course in précis-writing. It tells you exactly what a précis is and how the exercise of précis-writing can help you learn to write well, whether you are a student of English composition, translation, or English as a second language. The book includes theoretical background, practical step-by-step instructions on how to write a précis, some general guidelines, and some sample précis. It also provides a variety of exercises to give you hands-on experience as you become adept at précis-writing.

Précis-writing can be invaluable to English composition students—especially when it comes time to write a research paper. The skills you learn here can be used in most of your other courses—from simple essay writing to honours theses and graduate dissertations.

If you are a second-language student, précis-writing can help you develop a new way of looking at a text. It will help wean you away from word-by-word translations when reading texts in your second language, and help you develop an overall approach to the meaning of a discourse.

Acknowledgements

This book has been written during my years of teaching English writing techniques at the School of Translators and Interpreters of the University of Ottawa. I would like to thank my colleagues Roda Roberts, Jean Delisle, and Ingrid Meyer for their ongoing support and encouragement in this project. I am also grateful to Judith Woodsworth and Brenda Hosington for acting as readers, and to Wendy Quinlan-Gagnon for her editing work. I thank Toivo Roht and Janet Shorten of the University of Ottawa Press for their assistance in having this book published. Thanks also to my students for doing countless exercises and for sharing their comments and ideas, and in particular to past student assistants Carolyn Young and Patricia Wainwright. Lastly, thanks to my family—my parents Alexander Cameron Grant and Clare Grant, my husband Richard Caton, and my children Janna and Kristina Russell—for their unfailing support and understanding.

Acknowledgements are made to the following publishers who have given me permission to use extracts from their texts.

Time, for the article "Bye Columbus," in *Time*, August 18, 1980. Copyright 1980 Time Inc. All rights reserved. Reprinted by permission from *Time*.

Time, for the article "Treasure off Tsushima," in *Time*, October 20, 1980. Copyright 1980 Time Inc. All rights reserved. Reprinted by permission from *Time*.

Maclean's, for the article "No Exit for Entrance," by Suzanne Zwarun, in *Maclean's*, February 16, 1981. Reprinted by permission from the author.

Maclean's, for extracts from the article "Rabbits Do It but They Never Mow the Roof," by Mark Czarnecki, in *Maclean's*, February 25, 1980. Reprinted by permission from the author.

Maclean's, for the article "Divorced from a Generation," by Toba Korenblum, in *Maclean's*, June 2, 1980. Reprinted by permission from the author.

CNRC, for extracts from the article "Evidence from the Ocean Floor—Firming up Continental Drift," by Séan McCutcheon, in *Science Dimension*, Vol. 14, No. 4, 1982.

Environment Canada, for the article, "PCBs: An Environmental Nightmare," in *Land*, Vol. 8, No. 1, April 1987.

L'Express, for the article "Icare pour tous," by Jacques Potherat, in *L'Express*, No. 1671, July 22, 1983.

Le Nouvel Observateur, for extracts from the editorial "Comment parler d'autre chose?" by Jean Daniel in *Le Nouvel Observateur*, No. 752, April 9, 1979.

The Financial Post, for extracts from the article "Monetarism," by Michael Walker, in *The Financial Post*, February 28, 1981.

The University of Ottawa Press, for extracts from the following articles: "Hawking and Peddling in Canada, 1897-1914," by John Benson, in *Histoire sociale/Social History*, Vol. XVIII, No. 35, May 1985.

"Seventeen Reasons Why the Squatter Problem Can't Be Solved," by Shlomo Angel, in *The Southeast Asian Environment*, 1983.

"Satellite Broadcasting in Northern Canada," by Jean McNulty, in *Explorations in Canadian Economic History*, 1985.

"L'Afrique à la veille des invasions arabes," by C. M. Wells, in *University of Ottawa Quarterly*, January-March 1982.

"La continuité de l'emprise des compagnies de pêche françaises et jersiaises sur les pêcheurs au XVIIIᵉ siècle — Le cas de la compagnie Robin," by Mario Mimeault, in *Histoire sociale/Social History*, Vol. XVIII, No. 35, May 1985.

"Contemporary Ethical Issues Surrounding Electroconvulsive Therapy," by B. F. Hoffman, in *Psychiatric Journal of the University of Ottawa*, Vol. XI, No. 2, June-July 1986.

Introduction

The précis is a type of written summary, in narrative form, that accurately reflects the content of an original passage. It is primarily an academic exercise used to develop the student's ability to understand written material, to reformulate ideas succinctly, and to write well.

This manual is divided into two parts: Part One describes theory and methods, and Part Two consists of a selection of practical exercises.

Part One describes what the précis is and how it can be used in language teaching and testing. It includes theoretical background, practical step-by-step instructions for writing a précis, general guidelines, and a sample précis. Part One also includes two appendices that are designed specifically for English-language teachers. Appendix I gives teachers and markers some suggestions on marking and evaluating précis. Appendix II deals with the teaching of writing skills to translation students in particular, and is intended specifically for teachers of translation and others interested in the training of translators.

Part Two contains a collection of practical exercises. These exercises are divided into nine sections, and follow a logical progression. There are exercises on reading and comprehending texts, on analysing meaning and summarizing short passages, and on summarizing articles, instructions, correspondence, and speeches. For translation students and second-language students, there are exercises on writing précis in English of French texts. For advanced students, there are also sections on popularizing and abstracting. Some sections begin with samples that can be studied and discussed in class before the subsequent exercises are assigned.

Part One

CHAPTER 1

Brevity is the soul of wit. (William Shakespeare, *Hamlet*, II, ii)

What is a Précis?

DEFINING THE PRÉCIS

In a broad sense, the term "précis" can be defined as a summary—a summary of the contents of a document or series of documents, a summary of a series of events, or a summary of the proceedings of a meeting or conference.

However, the term is usually used in a more specialized way, to designate a particular type of summarizing exercise used for academic purposes. In this book, the word "précis" will be used in this more specialized sense: it will refer to a written text, of a prescribed length, that accurately summarizes a longer passage. The précis should accurately convey all the primary ideas of the original, omitting details and ideas of secondary importance. It should be written largely in terms other than those used in the original. It should be an uncommented text: it is not a critical review and must not express the précis-writer's opinions.

TYPES OF SUMMARIES

All types of summary-writing are based on the same general principles—the discrimination between essential and non-essential material, the judicious selection of key ideas, and the compilation of the essential information into a new text.

There are a variety of specialized forms of the summary—abstracts, précis, and abridgements, to name a few. Types of summaries vary primarily with respect to their *purpose*. A summary must be oriented towards its prospective audience, and the summary-writer, like the translator, must take into consideration the purpose of the exercise and the needs of the recipient of the target text. The précis, for example, is basically an academic exercise—hence the emphasis on the style and readability of the finished product as a piece of prose in its own right. Abstracts, on the other hand, are pragmatic texts designed to be used primarily by specialists interested in the content of recent publications in their field. As for abridgements, they often simplify as well as summarize material: the abridged texts that one finds in *Reader's Digest*, *Coles Notes*, or *Classic Comics* not only summarize but also popularize the original material and are designed for audiences who for a variety of reasons do not choose to tackle the original material.

It would be useful at this point to examine some of the varieties of summaries, thereby clarifying how précis-writing resembles, and differs from, other types of summary-writing.

The Précis

The précis has several distinctive features. First, it is usually of a prescribed length—in many cases, one-third of the length of the original. Moreover, in précis-writing, emphasis is placed on writing the summary *in terms other than* those used in the original, with the exception of a few key words or phrases. The précis thus combines the characteristics of the paraphrase and the summary: the précis should be a fluid text which stands on its own as an accurate, condensed re-creation of the source text, rather than a collage of expressions and sentences copied from the original. In précis-writing, the quality of original composition is an important factor.

This emphasis on original composition is understandable, since précis-writing is primarily an academic exercise. Précis-writing exercises have long been used in secondary schools and schools of higher learning to develop language and communication skills. In this context, the précis is of great educational value. On the one hand, it develops passive language skills—the ability to read intelligently, to detect the principal ideas and the pattern of thought in texts, and to become aware of the logic and quality of thought underlying a passage. On the other hand, it develops active language skills—the ability to use words effectively and to write clearly and precisely.

Furthermore, précis-writing is an excellent testing tool, and has been used as part of entrance examinations by colleges, universities, and civil services in countries such as Great Britain, France, and Canada. It enables examiners to evaluate not only the linguistic skills but also the general intellectual abilities of the candidates.

The Abstract

An abstract is a summary of the essential facts and theories presented in a report, article, or other document. "Author abstracts" are written by the author or publishing house and are published along with the document itself; "access abstracts" are written by information specialists and published in collections by abstracting services, or stored in computer memories.[1] Perhaps the best known collection of access abstracts is the voluminous collection called *Chemical Abstracts*.

These abstracting and indexing services have been established to deal with the enormous amount of literature being published and to help the individual scientist or specialist keep abreast of publications in his or her field. Thousands of abstracting services exist, covering fields such as science, technology, and the humanities.

Most libraries provide series of abstract journals containing abstracts of articles from a wide variety of fields. Most of these abstract journals are published on a regular basis (annually or even more frequently) and contain subject indexes; they thus provide a most efficient means for the specialist to gain access to a wide range of material. Interlingual abstracts allow researchers to learn what foreign-language documents are being published and to decide whether they want to have a document translated.

Abstracts are an integral part of library science and information analysis. As the field of computerized language processing has grown, progress has been made in developing automatic abstracting systems. Interestingly enough, a computerized subject indexing system used by the British National Bibliography is called PRECIS.

In *Abstracting Concepts and Methods*, Borko and Bernier describe the abstract as follows:

> An abstract is a well-defined type of literature with definite attributes and a unique style. Abstracting is not a 'natural' form of writing; it requires training. The abstract must be brief and accurate, and it must be presented in a format designed to facilitate the skimming of a large number of abstracts in a search for relevant material.[2]

There are two standard types of abstract, with two distinct functions. The descriptive, or indicative, abstract describes the scope of the text, but does not contain extensive data and is not designed to replace the original. Rather, it is designed to help the reader decide whether or not the original is relevant to his or her research. The second type of abstract, the informative abstract, gives more detailed information on the content of the article; it can in some cases replace the source text and save the reader the bother of reading the original document.

Particularly in the fields of science and technology, the abstract is theme-oriented: it focuses on specific topics in the original text. The descriptive abstract summarizes purpose and methodology, and the informative abstract summarizes purpose, methodology, observations, conclusions, and recommendations.

The Popularized Abridgement

Abridged versions of books are used as a means of popularizing literature. The child curls up with the *Classic Comic* of *David Copperfield*; the high-school student crams the night before the big test by reading the *Coles Notes* abridgement of *Romeo and Juliet;* the cottager keeps the bookshelves stacked with *Reader's Digest* versions of novels. Although reading a condensed version is not the same as savouring the original work in its entirety, these publications do introduce literary works to people who would perhaps never wade through the more lengthy and sophisticated originals. In today's world of TV dinners and convenience foods, the popularity of "instant" literature is not surprising.

Similarly, much technical and scientific information is disseminated in popularized form through articles written for the layman with a casual interest in a specialized field. In this popularization process, technical knowledge is condensed, simplified, and explained so that it can be understood by a broad non-specialized readership.

Summary Records of Proceedings

Many situations call for the summarizing of spoken material. Students take notes during lectures; journalists summarize speeches and statements; secretaries take minutes of meetings. In all these situations, the original material is presented in oral form, and the "reporter" makes notes during the proceedings in order to record the salient points.

Some organizations provide comprehensive summary reports of their proceedings. The United Nations uses the term "précis" to designate the summary records that it provides of meetings held by some of its various bodies. These summary records are prepared in the official languages in which the proceedings take place, and are subsequently translated into all the other official languages of the body concerned. These summary records should not be confused with minutes; they are more comprehensive than minutes, and constitute the official records of the bodies in question. These précis, or summary records, are drawn up by the UN translation services; thus summary-writing represents a substantial part of the work done by UN translators.

In other situations, such as UNESCO symposiums, the proceedings are printed in their entirety in the languages in which they are held, and translation-summaries are provided in the other relevant languages.

THE SUMMARY AS A SURROGATE TEXT

All the types of summaries that have been described are based on previously existing material. They are surrogate texts, as are the translation, the paraphrase, the excerpt, the review, and numerous other types of texts. Surrogate texts clearly vary with respect to their form and the nature of their relationships with their respective source texts, but they have in common the fact that they are target texts resulting from a transformation of source material. (In the case of the summary record, the source material is spoken rather than written.)

It would be useful to look at a few of these document surrogates[3] and see where the similarities and differences lie.

The "summary" is a condensed version of an original text. It is necessarily briefer than the original, and it contains only the main ideas of the source text.

The "translation" is a surrogate text which transfers an original message into another language. Translation is thus an interlingual process which requires the reformulation of the message in another linguistic system. The translated text should accurately reflect all the content of the original.

The "paraphrase" is a rewording of an original message in the same language as the original—a sort of intralingual translation.[4] It involves the systematic substitution of one lexical item, expression, or sentence for another, and the finished product closely resembles the original in structure and in length.

The "extract" or the "excerpt" is a portion of an original text that has been copied verbatim. Unlike the summary, it is not a scale model; rather, it reproduces segments of the original text as representative of the whole.

The "review" briefly describes the content of a text, but it also expresses the reviewer's opinion of the original. This element of subjective evaluation differentiates the review, and any form of literary criticism, from the objective summary.

There are numerous other types of surrogate texts that, like the ones described above, result from a transformation of source material. The task of comparing and contrasting types of surrogate texts requires a systematic approach. An excellent study of the nature of the "intertextuality of texts" can be found in H. Van Gorp's "La traduction littéraire parmi les autres métatextes".[5] Van Gorp uses Popovič's term "metatext"[6] to describe a text which refers to another text (called the "prototext"). All metatexts are related to previously existing material; Van Gorp points out that the same process of "lecture-écriture"[7] is involved in such activities as literary criticism, translation, summarizing, quotation, parody, adaptation, and even writing itself, and he goes on to examine the various possible relationships that can exist between prototexts and metatexts. He first distinguishes between three types of metatext: intralingual (quotations, summaries, commentaries, etc.), interlingual (translations), and intersemiotic (adaptations such as screenplays, illustrations, and comic strips). He then studies the nature of the transformation itself, and distinguishes between the processes of repetition (as seen in quotations, allusions, excerpts, and plagiarism), amplification (as seen in prologues, appendices, and literary criticism), suppression or reduction (which applies to summaries), and substitution (examples include paraphrase, adaptation, parody, and translation).

Using Van Gorp's terminology, the précis would fall into the category of intralingual metatext created through reduction, whereas the translation could be roughly described as an interlingual metatext created through substitution.[8]

---

1. The terms "author abstract" and "access abstract" are taken from Edward Cremmins' *The Art of Abstracting* (Philadelphia: ISI Press, 1982), p. 5.
2. Harold Borko and Charles Bernier, *Abstracting Concepts and Methods* (New York: Academic Press, 1975), p. 9.
3. The term "document surrogate" is used by Borko and Bernier in *Abstracting Concepts and Methods*, p. 5.
4. Paraphrasing and intralingual translation are discussed further in Part Two, Section 4 of this book. Also see Jean Delisle's description of "la traduction intralinguale" in his book *L'analyse du discours comme méthode de traduction* (Ottawa: University of Ottawa Press, 1980), pp. 204-206.
5. H. Van Gorp, "La traduction littéraire parmi les autres métatextes," in *Literature and Translation*, ed. James S. Holmes, José Lambert, and Raymond Van Den Broeck (Leuven, Belgium: Acco, 1978), pp. 101-116.
6. Anton Popovič, *Dictionary for the Analysis of Literary Translation* (Edmonton: University of Alberta, 1976), p. 30.
7. Van Gorp, "La traduction littéraire parmi les autres métatextes," p. 114.
8. I say "roughly" here because Van Gorp is careful to explain that these processes overlap and that translation can incorporate all of them.

CHAPTER 2

The most valuable of all talents is that of never using two words when one will do. (Thomas Jefferson)

How is the Précis Used?

HISTORICAL BACKGROUND

Summary-writing dates back almost to the beginning of the keeping of written records; man has always sought a means of briefly indicating the essence of a text. Précis-writing as a specific branch of summary-writing has developed more recently, and has evolved into its present form principally in the past century.

The summarizing of documents was practised even before books as we know them today existed. Detailed accounts can be found in Frank J. Witty's "The Beginnings of Indexing and Abstracting: Some Notes Toward a History of Indexing in Antiquity and the Middle Ages," in Borko and Bernier's *Abstracting Concepts and Methods*, and in Collison's *The Annals of Abstracting, 1665-1970*. According to Witty, summaries appeared "on some of the clay envelopes enclosing Mesopotamian cuneiform documents of the early second millennium B.C."[1] The contents of papyrus rolls, particularly those dealing with histories and plays, were summarized in the era of the great Alexandrian library. These early summaries sometimes contained subjective commentary and thus were not necessarily objective condensations.[2]

Borko and Bernier write:

> Many plays, of both the Greeks and the Romans, were preceded by . . . summaries, many of which were written in verse. The purposes of these ancient abstracts . . . were to provide concise information about the original document and to facilitate the search for, and recall of, specific information. It was also the custom to abstract

deeds of sale, contracts, and other like documents. In the Middle Ages, when monks transcribed manuscripts, they would frequently make marginalia that summarized the page's contents.[3]

Over the centuries, ambassadors' reports were condensed by royal secretaries for kings to read; the reports of papal envoys were summarized for popes. Later, Elizabethan scientists prepared and distributed summaries of their projects in order to disseminate the knowledge they had acquired.[4]

Abstracting, as a specific type of summarizing, took on a more structured form in 1665, when the first abstract periodical, *Le Journal des Sçavans*, was published. German and British abstract journals appeared in the eighteenth century, and by the nineteenth century, a wide variety of abstract periodicals was being published. The publication of abstracts has mushroomed since that time. Summarizing in general thus evolved largely as a means of communication and dissemination of information.

Précis-writing, as a specialized type of summarizing, was developed mainly for two purposes: as a means of teaching language skills, and as a means of testing people's linguistic and intellectual abilities.

As a means of teaching language skills, précis-writing was used in secondary schools and schools of higher learning in the nineteenth century (and perhaps earlier), although the term "précis" was initially used in a broader sense than it is today. At the beginning of the twentieth century in Britain, the précis often consisted of a condensation and synthesis of information contained in a series of letters or other documents; often the précis was one-twentieth of the length of the original. During the twentieth century, the concept of exactly what a précis is has changed somewhat, although the basic principles behind the exercise remain the same. Many English grammar and composition textbooks published today contain sections on précis-writing, and they usually describe the précis as a narrative summary of a text, one-third of the length of the original.

The use of the précis as an examination exercise in nineteenth and early twentieth century Britain is described by Jackson and Briggs in *A Text-book of Précis-Writing*. Around the turn of the century, the précis was used as an exercise in the College of Preceptors' examinations, the Oxford Local Examination for Commercial Certificates, and Civil Service Exams for Clerkships and Excise. In 1902, it was adopted as part of the London Matriculation Examination and the Society of Arts Examination. Jackson and Briggs include in their book the instructions from the London Matriculation Examination of September 1902:

> Write out in your own words a précis of the following letters, which relate to the appointment of Lord Malmesbury, in 1796, as our plenipotentiary in Paris, and to his negotiations with the Directory. The précis should give in a concise form a continuous narrative, readily intelligible without reference to the original documents, embracing the essential facts and those only.[5]

Today, the précis continues to play the dual role of teaching tool and testing tool. The remainder of this chapter will examine the present-day uses of the précis.

PRÉCIS-WRITING AND TESTING

Summarizing has many applications in the field of testing and evaluating intellectual and linguistic ability. In the book *La contraction et la synthèse de textes*, author Jean Moreau states that the exercise of writing a summary tests an applicant's intelligence, general knowledge, judgement, and ability to express ideas. It has been widely used in France as part of entrance examinations to various schools of higher learning, including the École centrale des arts et manufactures, the INS de chimie industrielle de Rouen, the École navale, the École vétérinaire, the École nationale su-

périeure agronomique de Nancy, and the Écoles supérieures de commerce et d'administration.[6] Of course, texts on specific topics can be chosen in order to test the applicant's knowledge and understanding of a particular field.

Précis-writing is obviously a suitable exercise for testing applicants to language programs. Précis-writing skills are particularly indicative of a person's potential ability in the field of translation. Knowledge of two languages in no way guarantees a person's suitability for translation; certain intellectual inclinations are also required. The quality of a précis can indicate whether or not the applicant possesses the abilities required in translation: objectivity, logic, and the ability to comprehend, analyse, and express ideas—to process information. As Peter Newmark writes, "In many respects, ability to précis corresponds to the 'organisational' (as opposed to the fantasy or lateral) aspect of intelligence."[7]

Précis-writing is an important part of the entrance examinations at the School of Translators and Interpreters at the University of Ottawa. Applicants to the three-year undergraduate program are asked to summarize a short text in several sentences, whereas applicants to the more advanced programs are given the more rigorous task of writing a précis *per se*, with the exact length of the précis prescribed. At the undergraduate level, the summarizing test is given in conjunction with tests of grammar, vocabulary, composition, comprehension, and general knowledge; at the more advanced levels, précis-writing tests are given in conjunction with paraphrasing and translation tests.

PRÉCIS-WRITING AND LANGUAGE TEACHING

Précis-writing is taught in a variety of types of language courses. Whether you are a student of English composition, English as a second language, or translation, précis-writing can help you to improve your language and communication skills.

At the secondary school level, traditional précis-writing is often a component of first-language composition courses. The exercise provides the teacher with a vehicle to teach writing skills within a controlled framework. Thus many English-language grammar books contain elementary exercises on précis-writing.

But précis-writing is not limited to secondary school composition courses; it can play an important role in a wide variety of communication and business writing courses as a means of polishing writing techniques and information processing skills. It has the advantage of developing passive language skills (reading and comprehension) as well as active language skills (writing and expressing ideas).

Précis-writing can be a useful component of second-language courses as well. In second-language courses, the précis need not necessarily take an intralingual form: in addition to writing summaries of second-language texts in that second language, you can précis in your mother tongue a text written in your second language (as a means of developing your ability to understand the second language), or you can précis in the second language a text written in your mother tongue (as a means of developing your ability to express yourself in the second language).

Précis-writing is particularly valuable as a component of translator training programs. It is taught in a number of translator training schools, either as a separate course (for example, at the Université de Montréal, Laurentian University, and the London Polytechnic), or as part of a general writing skills course for translators (for example, at the University of Ottawa and at the University of Moncton). The following section will examine the role of précis-writing in translator training programs.

PRÉCIS-WRITING AND TRANSLATOR TRAINING

Translation, like composition, can be neither taught nor learned solely from theory: it is an *applied* discipline. It is a skill to master, not simply a body of knowledge to acquire. The need to develop this skill *by doing* is the reason for the practical nature of translator training programs.

What are the components of a translator training program? Of course, the program should contain courses in practical translation, but it should also include courses in subjects such as documentation, research, terminology, comparative stylistics, and writing skills. Let us look specifically at the writing skills component.

Many people are fluent in two or more languages, yet are unable to write well. Writing skills courses should ensure that the would-be translator can write well in all the languages he or she will work with, but particularly in the target language. A translator is a writer, and will never be a really good translator if not a proficient writer.

The would-be translator must therefore learn to write competently. A natural place to begin is with grammar. There are many grammar books in print, and mastering the rules of grammar is a fairly straightforward task: such points as subject-verb agreement, parallel structure, capitalization, and punctuation are fairly basic. But where do you go from there? There is a vast difference between simply writing without making grammatical errors, and actually writing well. A text may be free of grammatical errors and errors of usage, yet it may be stylistically mediocre (for example, it could be made up of short, choppy sentences or could contain hackneyed vocabulary), or it may present ideas in an illogical or incoherent manner. Such a text should not be considered acceptable simply because it is "error-free." Ideas must be presented clearly, coherently, and effectively, and the writing style must be polished. The ability to put thoughts into words and to put words and sentences together in an intelligent and pleasing manner is not easily developed.

Yet if you want to be a translator, you must learn all this, and even more. You must also acquire writing skills that are applicable to the profession of translator. Let us examine those aspects of linguistic competence that should be stressed.

First, you must learn to reformulate meaning. The writing skills needed in translation are not the same as those needed in creative writing. Rather than "creating," the translator "re-creates"; therefore, exercises that involve "re-creating" a text are particularly useful in translator training. Language courses in a translation program should not concentrate on creative writing—although creative writing does have a place, especially for those interested in literary and poetic translation (an aspect of translation that is overlooked in many translation programs, since job opportunities in the literary field are few). Rather, the training should focus on pragmatic writing and the transmission of information for the purpose of communication.

Since the précis itself is a reformulation of an original text, the exercise of précis-writing is particularly well suited to writing skills courses for translators. Précis-writing develops the ability to extract the basic message and structure from a text—to grasp meaning quickly. It teaches you an analytical approach to source material and develops your ability to distinguish thought patterns and to organize ideas. It teaches you to express specific ideas without wasting words, thus developing your ability to use words effectively and to put your finger on the elusive *mot juste*. It also helps you develop insight into accuracy and distortion in information transfer.

A second aspect of linguistic competence that a would-be translator needs to develop is the ability to work with texts. Traditional grammar and language courses tend to focus on particular sentence structures and limited contexts rather than texts, and to stress *langue* rather than *parole*. Yet the translator works with texts; as Jean Delisle writes:

> Le texte est une entité significative beaucoup plus riche que la phrase et on ne traduit jamais des phrases, mais toujours des textes.[8]

Précis-writing is a textually oriented exercise. The task of summarizing obliges you to consider the text as a unit. Because of the linear, consecutive nature of language, too much emphasis can be placed on the word, and too little on the message. By focusing your attention on the meaning of the text as a whole, précis-writing helps train you to view a text as a message, and the individual words and expressions, as parts of that message. In other words, the exercise forces you to adopt a contextual rather than a linear approach to the source text; it emphasizes logic rather than syntax.

It is tempting to pick up an assigned text and, with scarcely a glance at the body of the passage, begin to translate the first line. Despite repeated pleadings from instructors, you may fall prey to the urge to "translate first, read later." You may subsequently run into specific problems because you are unable to see the forest for the trees. Can you imagine how difficult it would be to try to piece together a jigsaw puzzle without having a clear idea of what the completed picture should look like? Yet this is similar to the task of translating an expression without having an understanding of the purpose and meaning of the text in which it occurs. The translator does not simply replace a series of terms with a series of equivalents: rather, he or she tries to reconstruct a "pattern of meaning"[9] and to relay a message from the author to the reader. Like the person who fits together a jigsaw puzzle by referring to an image of the finished product, the translator determines the intended meaning of a term or expression by considering its role within a larger context.

Because précis-writing cannot be accomplished without contextual analysis, it trains you to think of meaning in terms of context.[10] Since it also trains you to write well, to think clearly, and to reformulate meaning accurately, it is an exercise admirably suited to translator training.

BEYOND THE TRADITIONAL PRÉCIS: VARIATIONS OF SUMMARY-WRITING EXERCISES

Variations of the Intralingual Précis

The standard intralingual précis can take a variety of forms. The degree of condensation required can vary enormously: you could be asked to condense a text to one-third, one-fifth, one-tenth or one-twentieth of its original length, or to summarize it in a given number of words. The scale may vary, but the method remains the same.

Source texts need not be limited to short articles; you can summarize entire books. For example, in first-year English courses at the École d'Interprètes Internationaux de l'Université de l'État à Mons, students are given a reading list of ten books, and are required to present summaries of these books during the term.[11] This type of exercise has the added benefit of exposing students to the literature of a particular language.

The Interlingual Précis

An excellent exercise in a translation or second-language course is to write a translation-summary, in which you summarize the source text in a specific number of words in a second language. This exercise combines translation and précis-writing skills. The following diagram compares the relationship between source and target texts in translation, intralingual précis-writing, and interlingual précis-writing.

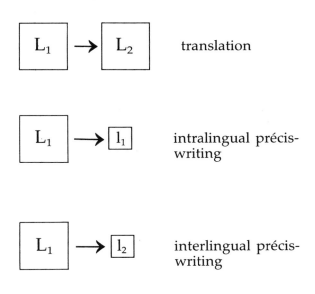

$L_1 \rightarrow L_2$ translation

$L_1 \rightarrow l_1$ intralingual précis-writing

$L_1 \rightarrow l_2$ interlingual précis-writing

Translation-summaries can be done for professional as well as for academic purposes. English-language abstracts of foreign-language scientific and technical papers are one example of the application of the translation-summary.

The Summary Record

Another useful exercise for developing your language skills is to prepare a summary from spoken source material. For example, your teacher may read a text aloud to the class and ask you to take notes and prepare a summary—either an oral synopsis, or a written summary to be handed in for correction. As an alternative, you could be required to attend a lecture or conference and subsequently submit a report of it. This exercise can take either an intralingual or an interlingual form. In its intralingual form, it develops listening and note-taking skills. In its interlingual form, it has much in common with consecutive interpretation,[12] and is a good introduction for students planning to study interpretation. In either form, you must analyse and dissect the discourse as it is read or spoken, recognize principal ideas, and group subordinate ideas around them. In *La prise de notes en interprétation consécutive*, Jean-François Rozan describes a technique of note-taking for consecutive interpretation. By focusing on the ideas, not the words—on *le fond, non la forme*[13]—you can recognize the hierarchy of ideas and can trace the organization and development of the mes-

sage through the use of symbols and the grouping of these symbols. A consecutive interpreter does not have time to write down entire sentences, and so is forced to reduce the discourse to its essence. Such an exercise brings to light the logical structure of a discourse, including main themes, connections between ideas, repetition, and parallelism of meaning.

The Synthesis-Summary

The writing of a synthesis-summary is another related exercise. In drawing up a synthesis of two or more articles on a particular topic, you must first grasp the main ideas in each of the articles, and then combine the material into one concise comprehensive text.

Jean Moreau discusses techniques of synthesis and provides examples and exercises in his book *La contraction et la synthèse de textes*. Moreau explains that it is inadequate to simply summarize each text separately or compare the texts; rather, you must look for common themes and then logically redistribute the content of the texts among these themes.[14]

Yves Stalloni also describes a method for producing a synthesis-summary in his book *Méthode de contraction et de synthèse de textes*. Stalloni suggests that you make a separate outline for each text in order to identify the major ideas of each author, and then integrate these ideas by drawing up an outline for your synthesis, which should be based on common themes and should reveal similarities and differences in the author's opinions.[15]

The Abstract

Writing skills courses can also include the drawing up of abstracts for articles or reports. Writing abstracts of technical articles in particular helps "demystify" the field of technical writing and is good training for technical writers and technical translators.

Abstracts are a very specialized type of summary with a specific format. The standard length of an abstract is 100-250 words, depending on the length and complexity of the original. The most common type of abstract describes a technical or scientific report, and has a recognizable pattern, focusing on set themes—purpose, methodology, results, conclusions, and recommendations.

Standard rules and conventions for writing abstracts have been set out in various publications, notably the American National Standards Institute's *American National Standard for Writing Abstracts*. An excellent description of how the abstractor should go about drawing up an abstract is given in Cremmins' *The Art of Abstracting*. Moreover, many abstracting services publish instruction sheets and manuals for their abstractors, outlining "house" rules and conventions. Courses in abstracting are sometimes given as part of information-science and library-science programs.

In Section 9 of Part Two of this book, you can find guidelines for writing abstracts, a sample abstract, and an abstracting exercise.

---

1. Frank J. Witty, "The Beginnings of Indexing and Abstracting: Some Notes Toward a History of Indexing in Antiquity and the Middle Ages," *The Indexer*, Vol. 8, No. 4, October 1973, p. 193.
2. Borko and Bernier, *Abstracting Concepts and Methods*, p. 26.
3. *Ibid.*, p. 27.
4. *Ibid.*, p. 28.
5. Jackson and Briggs, *A Text-book of Précis-Writing*, p. 91.
6. Jean Moreau, *La contraction et la synthèse de textes* (Paris: Éditions Fernand Nathan, 1977), pp. 7, 22, 26.
7. Peter Newmark, "In Defence of the Précis," in *The Use of English*, No. 25/3, Spring 1974, p. 226.
8. Jean Delisle, *L'analyse du discours comme méthode de traduction* (Ottawa: University of Ottawa Press, 1980), p. 123.
9. In lectures on translation, Brian Mossop has emphasized the importance of grasping the pattern of meaning of a text and seeing the individual elements as partial expressions of this pattern. In his words, "Grasping the pattern of meaning frees one from the tyranny of the words of the original."
10. For a study of the meaning of the term "context" and the importance of context in translation, see Roda P. Roberts, "Context in Translation," in *Actes du 10e Colloque de l'ACLA*, May 1979, pp. 117-132.
11. E. Koberski, "A Contribution to the Training of Translators: Précis-Writing in the First Year English Syllabus Explored," in *Vingt ans d'enseignement et de recherche en traduction et en interprétation de conférence* (Mons: Université de Mons, Hainaut, 1983), pp. 177-180.
12. Consecutive interpretation involves the interpreter taking notes during the discourse and delivering the interpretation afterwards, as opposed to simultaneous interpretation, in which the interpreter orally translates the discourse as it is given.
13. Jean-François Rozan, *La prise de notes en interprétation consécutive* (Geneva: Librairie de l'Université Georg, 1965), p. 27.
14. Jean Moreau, *La contraction et la synthèse de textes*, p. 112.
15. Yves Stalloni, *Méthode de contraction et de synthèse de textes* (Paris: Ellipses, 1981), pp. 138-141.

CHAPTER 3

Order is Heaven's first law.
(Alexander Pope)

C'est en s'efforçant de parler avec précision qu'on apprend à penser avec justesse. (Sainte Beuve, quoted by Boret and Peyrot)

How Do You Write a Précis?

A FIVE-STEP APPROACH

How exactly do you write a précis? The best results are achieved by taking a systematic approach to the exercise.[1] The process can be broken down into five basic steps: 1) reading and understanding the text; 2) analysing the content; 3) selecting and compressing important material; 4) preparing the draft précis; and 5) revising the précis.

Reading and Understanding the Text

The first step in précis-writing is obviously to gain a thorough understanding of the original text. Many people read carelessly; in first attempts at précis-writing, ideas are often added, omitted, or distorted. The first step thus entails reading the text carefully for comprehension. You must not only understand all details, allusions, and terms; you must also have a clear view of the text as a whole. An overall grasp can be attained by asking questions such as: What is the purpose of this text—is the author trying to inform, describe, persuade, explain, narrate, entertain, or amuse? What is the author's attitude? Does the author express a personal point of view, or is the text purely objective? Is there a distinctive style or tone to the text?

At this point it would be useful to define the terms "style" and "tone" as used in this book:

Style: a characteristic manner of expression, combining the idea that is being expressed with the individuality of the author. A work could be categorized as written in literary, journalistic, or scientific style. It could also be classified as abstract or concrete, formal or informal, original or imitative. Qualities such as diction, sentence structure and variety, imagery, rhythm, coherence and emphasis are elements of style.[2]

Tone: a manner of writing that shows a certain attitude on the part of the writer[3]—for example, a work could be described as having a friendly, sarcastic, sincere, or artificial tone.

Analysing the Content

Once you have understood and digested the original text, the next step is to analyse the content.[4] This analysis involves studying the manner in which the ideas are presented and determining the underlying structure of the text. You should try to draw up an outline representing the organization and development of the ideas in the text. Some texts are more highly structured than others, but all have some sort of structure. When you are analysing a text, a paragraph-by-paragraph approach is usually helpful. As you trace the progression of the author's ideas, bear in mind the theme and purpose of the whole text, and ask yourself how each part is related to the overall message. There are many possible types of structural development of texts—for example, the author might recount a chronological sequence of events, describe a scene, compare or contrast ideas, make a general statement and support it with particulars, or use a combination of these and other approaches. Whatever the structure of the original, reconstruct it in outline form.

Selecting and Compressing Important Material

The third step follows naturally from the second: as you analyse the content, weighing the relevance of each section and determining how it fits into the general pattern of thought, you will notice that some ideas are of primary importance, and others of secondary importance. This discrimination between essential and nonessential material is a crucial step and an invaluable exercise in judgement, logic, and common sense.

You cannot separate the selection of important ideas from the compression of content. Sometimes an idea, succinctly expressed in the original, can be transplanted into the précis with little alteration required. Much more often, however, the meaning lies on a deep rather than a surface level, and it must be extracted by compression of thought.

In some structures, a primary idea might be explicitly worded, surrounded by details like china packed in excelsior. In such a case, the basic information can be easily extracted. For example, by a simple pruning process you can reduce:

> The Ivory Coast is the world's leading exporter of cocoa (much of which is grown in Ghana), the third largest exporter of coffee, and, thanks to its forests and modern ports, a principal supplier of timber to Europe.

to: The Ivory Coast, a leading exporter of cocoa, coffee, and timber, . . .

Often, however, summarizing requires the use of terms other than those used in the original. For example, if a text were to describe a region as being the site of oil refineries, automobile plants, pulp and paper mills, and various small factories, you could call the region "industrialized." Similarly, if a person were described as having spoken French and English since childhood, having a good command of Spanish, and speaking German and Italian haltingly, you could summarize the information by calling the person "multilingual." In this type of reduction you do not simply choose terms from the original text; rather, you must come up with a new term that captures the underlying meaning.

Underlining words is recommended in some manuals as a technique for selecting key ideas in précis-writing. It can be useful to a certain extent: the passage may contain a few words, expressions, or sentences that should be highlighted. Yet underlining specific expressions is only a first step with many limitations—often the meaning lies behind, not within, the words. A whole attitude or impression may be transmitted implicitly rather than explicitly.

The preceding examples illustrate reduction on a very small scale—the condensation of small units of thought. However, a text must be viewed as a whole, an intricate fabric of interwoven ideas. Rather than adopting a word-by-word or even a sentence-by-sentence approach, you must focus on the overall message and view units of thought in light of their context. Importance is relative; a particular idea is weighed in comparison with the import of those around it.

Preparing the Draft Précis

Once you have extracted and compressed the essential material, it is time to draw up a draft précis. Usually your text will follow the same pattern of ideas as the original. Occasionally you may feel that rearranging the presentation of ideas will help clarify and condense the material. Such a change of presentation is acceptable when justified, but you must carry it out with skill and intelligence in order not to distort the message.

In writing the draft, strive to be faithful to the meaning of the original, yet at the same time to create a new passage. The précis should be an original composition, not a collage of sections of the source text.

As you draw up the précis, keep in mind the principle of brevity. Avoid wordy expressions, needless repetition, and circumlocutions. Select your vocabulary intelligently: a few well-chosen words can convey more information than reams of jargon. The rigorous demands of the word count leave no room for verbosity: each word counts (and is counted!) and thus must make a contribution to the message.

If the first draft is too long, you can reduce it in several ways. Perhaps you could convey the same information in fewer words by substituting shorter expressions for longer ones and by rephrasing ideas more succinctly. Or perhaps you have included nonessential ideas and should reexamine the content. A clear understanding of the pattern of thought in the original will enable you to decide if further cuts should be made.

Revising the Précis

You should revise the draft précis with several points in mind. Check for omissions and inaccuracies by reading over the original, sentence by sentence, and ensuring that all important information has been presented in the précis without distortion. Ask yourself whether the précis reflects not only the content but also the purpose and tone of the original. Check your composition, ensuring that your text is clear and contains no errors of grammar, usage, spelling, or punctuation.

You are well advised to do assignments—whether compositions, précis, or translations—well ahead of time so that you can put your work aside for a few hours—or if possible a few days—and then reread it with a fresh outlook. It is hard to approach a piece of writing with a clear perspective after having laboured and struggled with it for hours. You may find that words which are on the tip of your tongue but refuse to flow from the tip of your pen will spring forth spontaneously at a later reading. Also, after a settling period, you can pick up and read a précis, or a translation, as a unit separate from the original. Approaching a finished text as a passage which must stand on its own may bring to light unclear or incomplete sections of the target text which are difficult to pick out through bleary eyes thoroughly steeped in the original.

APPLYING THE PRÉCIS-WRITING PROCESS: A SAMPLE PRÉCIS

This section will illustrate how the five-step approach can be applied to a particular text.

Source Text

To the Chinese, Columbus has never been much of a hero. Three years ago, a Chinese historical journal denounced him as a "colonial pirate," for setting sail to pillage Asia. Now a Chinese scholar is claiming that Columbus may have been beaten to the New World by a fifth-century Buddhist monk named Huishen.

Sinologists have long known of the monk's voyage to a mysterious land called Fusang. But its location has been a source of contention. So has the veracity of his tales, which were questioned even by his contemporaries. Still, some modern scholars say Fusang could have been real, perhaps Japan or even the Pacific Coast of North America.

In the latest issue of the official magazine *China Reconstructs*, Maritime Historian Fang Zhongpu purports to solve the puzzle. His prime evidence: a 35 kg (80 lb.) doughnut-shaped stone discovered in 1972 off Point Conception, near Santa Barbara, California. Fang says that the stone is a clear sign of a pre-Columbian Chinese visitation, and he cites the testimony of some American scientists to back him. Roland Von Huene, the U.S. Geological Survey marine geologist who first spotted the curious object, recalls: "The center hole had clearly been made by tools." James Moriarty, a University of San Diego marine archaeologist, identifies it as a so-called messenger stone, probably of ancient Chinese origin. Such a stone could be sent sliding down an anchor chain, via the hole, to strip away accumulation of seaweed. Another stony relic, discovered five years ago off Los Angeles by two sports divers, Wayne Baldwin and Robert Miestrell, also hints at an early Chinese presence. To Moriarty and his assistant, Archaeologist Larry Pierson, it looks very much like the type of millstone known to have been used by Chinese sailors as anchors.

Other scholars are not so sure. USGS Mineralogist Ching Chang Woo, who was born in Canton, tried to date the messenger stone from its mineral crust, but could not do so because the sea deposits such materials at varying rates. Former UCLA Archaeologist William Clewlow allows that the stones are enticing bits of evidence, but "just aren't conclusive."

Fang is far more positive. By the third century A.D., he notes, Chinese merchant seamen had reached the Indian Ocean and could reckon their sailing speeds and distances. "So it would have been quite possible for Chinese ships to cross the Pacific in the fifth century."

Time
August 18, 1980
396 words

Step 1—Reading and Understanding the Text

The purpose of this text is informative: the writer describes a Chinese scholar's claim that a fifth-century monk discovered North America centuries before Columbus, and he gives evidence to support the theory. The article contains numerous facts and names. It is straightforward and easy to understand, contains no highly specialized terms, and is aimed at a general reading public. The style is a journalistic one: the writer is objective, reporting facts and conflicting opinions without supporting or attacking one particular stand.

Step 2—Analysing the Content

The following is a sentence-by-sentence, paragraph-by-paragraph analysis of the development of ideas within this text.

Paragraph 1 **Purpose**: To introduce the topic.
Central idea: A Chinese scholar claims that a fifth-century monk may have reached the New World long before Columbus did.
Development: Sentence 3 is the real topic sentence of the passage. The first two sentences are a lead-in, using the references to Columbus as a way of drawing the reader into the story and highlighting the significance of Fang's claim.

Paragraph 2 **Purpose**: To give historical background.
Central idea: There have long been tales of a monk's voyage to Fusang, an unknown land which may possibly have been North America.
Development: In sentence 4, the writer mentions tales of the monk's voyage to Fusang. Sentences 5 and 6 throw

some doubt on the veracity of the tales. Sentence 7 ties these tales in with the main theme and reinforces the notion that Fang's claim may be true.

Paragraph 3 **Purpose**: To describe discoveries which support Fang's claim.
Central idea: Two stone relics found off the California coast have been identified as possibly being of ancient Chinese origin.
Development: Sentence 8 gives more information about the Chinese scholar and his claim. Sentences 9 to 13 discuss his principal piece of evidence; and sentences 14 and 15 describe the second relic.

Paragraph 4 **Purpose**: To present views which cast doubt on the veracity of Fang's claim.
Central idea: Some scholars feel the two stones do not constitute conclusive evidence.
Development: Sentence 16 provides a transition: it warns that dissenting opinions exist. Sentences 17 and 18 state that two other scholars question Fang's claim.

Paragraph 5 **Purpose**: To present more support for Fang's claim.
Central idea: Fang asserts that Chinese seamen had the navigational know-how at that time to have been able to have made such a voyage.
Development: Sentence 19 provides a transition and reaffirms Fang's claim. Sentences 20 and 21 give additional support.

Step 3—Selecting and Compressing Important Material

The major ideas in the text can be summarized as follows:
1. Fang's theory: that a Buddhist monk reached North America in the fifth century.
2. Background: the legend
3. Evidence:
   3.1. Relics found

        3.1.1. messenger stone
        3.1.2. millstone
    3.2. Ancient Chinese sailing expertise
4. Dissenting views

Step 4—Preparing the Draft Précis

Here are some examples of distortions and inaccuracies that cropped up in carelessly written précis:

1. Columbus may lose his status as a hero if it can be proven that Huishen, a fifth-century Buddhist monk, was the first to find the New World. (distortion of fact)
2. Historian Fang Zhongpu found a doughnut-shaped stone which he believes was carved by tools. (distortion of fact)
3. Recently, the Chinese have come up with proof that contradicts the fact that Christopher Columbus was the first to set sail to the New World. (incorrect wording; distortion of fact)
4. Some US scientists believe that this proves some sort of visitation by the Chinese to America, but the evidence is insufficient. Fang's claim has a basic weakness: it lacks substantial evidence. (slanted opinion)

Organizing the Draft

While drawing up the draft, you might consider grouping the ideas according to the sequence given in Step 3. In this précis, however, the ideas should preferably be presented in the same sequence as in the original, for ending the passage by stating the dissenting views would leave the reader with a sceptical impression of the story.

Step 5—Revising the Précis

Here is a sample final version of a précis of this text.

A Chinese historian, Fang Zhongpu, has claimed that a fifth-century monk reached the New World centuries before Columbus did. An old legend, which Fang believes to be true, tells of the monk's travels to an unknown land, which might have been the Pacific coast of North America. Fang's evidence includes two stone relics found off the California coast, and the supporting testimony of several American scientists. The first relic has been identified as a messenger stone, quite possibly of ancient Chinese origin; the second appears to be the kind of millstone that Chinese seamen used to use. Fang is undaunted by criticism from some scholars that his evidence is inconclusive; he contends that early Chinese sailors had the navigational skills required for such a voyage.

124 words

---

1. This approach has been described previously in Pamela Russell's article, "The Importance of Précis-Writing in a Translator Training Programme," in *L'enseignement de l'interprétation et de la traduction: de la théorie à la pédagogie* (Ottawa: University of Ottawa Press, 1981).
2. Coles Editorial Board, *Dictionary of Literary Terms* (Toronto: Coles, 1980), p. 194.
3. *Webster's New Twentieth Century Dictionary* (New York: The World Publishing Co., 1974).
4. Descriptions of techniques used in understanding and analysing the meaning of texts can be found in Jean Delisle's *L'analyse du discours comme méthode de traduction*, and in Bernard Gicquel's *L'explication de textes et la dissertation* (Paris: Presses Universitaires de France, 1979). An English-language text that contains numerous exercises on comprehension is Linda Markstein and Louise Hirasawa's *Expanding Reading Skills, Advanced* (Rowley, Mass.: Newbury House Publishers, 1977).

CHAPTER 4

I hope you will pardon me for writing a long letter, but I did not have time to write a shorter one. (Translation of Blaise Pascal in *Lettres Provinciales*)

Inside or between languages, human communication equals translation. (George Steiner, *After Babel*, p. 47)

Guidelines For Précis-Writing

METHODS OF SHORTENING

The following section contains some general suggestions for shortening texts. However, these suggestions must be applied with judgement and discrimination; generalizations can be dangerous, and each text must be dealt with on an individual basis.

Lengthy lists and enumerations can often be summarized by the use of generic terms. It is far better to find one general term to summarize a series than to select one item in the series to represent the whole. For example, it is more accurate to reduce the sentence, "On weekends she makes pottery using her own kiln, does quilting, crochets afghans for her friends, and batiks," to "On weekends she does crafts," rather than to "On weekends she makes pottery." Similarly, "Representatives of the Liberal Party, the Progressive Conservative Party, and the New Democratic Party were in attendance," should be reduced to "Representatives of the major political parties were present," rather than to "Representatives of the Liberal Party were present."

Detailed descriptions, illustrations, and examples can often be omitted. In the sentence, "Almost any solid object offers an easier path for electricity than does air: it could be a tree, a utility pole, a high patch of ground, a barn, an outbuilding, or a house," the main idea is expressed in the first part of the sentence, and the list of examples of "solid objects" can be dropped.

Metaphors, similes, and picturesque discourse can often be reduced to a neutral form, unless the image is essential to the passage. For example, "He is socially inept," is a succinct way of expressing the meaning of the sentence, "When you see him out at a social event, you have to wonder if he were born in a barn." "She clucked about like an old hen who couldn't find her chicks," might be reduced to "She fussed about," or "She was flustered."

Repetition should be avoided; if repetition is used in the original text for emphasis, you could convey the emphasis by other means, such as by using emphatic vocabulary. Redundancies, such as "to vacillate back and forth" or "to look back in retrospect," should be avoided. Similarly, circumlocutions have no place in the précis, or in any good writing for that matter. "Approximately" is preferable to "in the neighbourhood of"; "because," to "in view of the fact that"; "if," to "in the event that"; and "therefore," to "with the result that."

Certain sentence structures are wordier than others. For example, subordinate clauses can often be reduced to shorter structures with no loss of meaning: "Peter, who was in a hurry to leave, was brusque," can be shortened to "Peter, anxious to leave, was brusque," and "Japanese leaders did not expect that their cities would be bombed and that their navy would be destroyed," can be shortened to "Japanese leaders did not expect their cities to be bombed and their navy destroyed." Similarly, parallel structures can often be shortened by the omission of common elements or by ellipsis: "He wanted to expand his horizons; he wanted to meet new people; he wanted to realize his potential," can be shortened to "He wanted to expand his horizons, meet new people, and realize his potential."

It is important to realize that the précis need not reduce every section of the original text to the same degree. A balanced précis reduces each section according to the relative importance of the ideas contained therein, not according to the number of words used in a particular section. For example, the introduction of a text is likely to contain important ideas and thus should be reduced to a lesser degree than other sections; similarly, the first sentence of a paragraph may well carry more weight than the descriptive or illustrative material following it. As Boret and Peyrot write,

> La réduction néanmoins n'est pas automatiquement proportionnelle à la longueur de chaque partie du texte original, comme ce serait le cas dans une réduction photographique.[1]

The following paragraph and its summary will serve as an illustration. Notice that, in the summary, the first sentence of the original paragraph is given considerably more weight than the subsequent sentences.

Original The first principle of a modern plan for traffic is to separate through traffic from local traffic. The American Automobile Association has said that from one-half to three-quarters of the automobiles in the downtown area have destinations elsewhere and are simply passing through because no convenient alternative route exists. It is short-sighted of business firms to insist upon having major arteries pass their doors. Through traffic discourages local people from driving downtown to shop.

The Royal Bank Letter,
Royal Bank of Canada

Summary A good traffic plan must first separate through traffic from local traffic. Through traffic, which reportedly accounts for the majority of traffic in city cores, deters local customers from frequenting downtown businesses.

REPORTING SPEECH

In many texts, the problem of reporting direct speech never arises; the original text is written in the third person, and you can naturally write from the original author's perspective. However, when summarizing speeches, autobiographical material, or other texts written in the first person, you are faced with a choice of approaches: you can put yourself in the shoes of the speaker and use the first person, or you can adapt your summary and report the ideas from the perspective of a listener. In the first case, your attitude is similar to that of the translator or the interpreter: you speak for the original author and your role is an "invisible" one. In the second case, you become a reporter and distance yourself from the original author. The second approach is the common one in précis-writing, and is the one recommended in this manual. This approach does entail some major changes in the material you are working with. You must convert direct speech to indirect speech, and first-person pronouns to third-person pronouns. As well, some changes of verb tense are necessary: for example, the present and future tenses may be changed to the past and the conditional respectively. "I promise that I will be there," might become "He promised that he would be there," or preferably "He promised to be there." Moreover, adverbial expressions of time need to be adapted accordingly: "I have arranged to examine the situation tomorrow" might be changed to "She had arranged to examine the situation on the following day." Similarly, "today" becomes "that day," and "next week," "the following week."

Adapting direct speech to indirect speech can be tricky. An excellent description of techniques for reporting speech can be found in Chapter 29 of A. J. Thomson and A. V. Martinet's, *A Practical English Grammar*.[2]

Section 7 of Part Two of this book contains a sample summary record and exercises on summarizing speeches; be sure to make the necessary changes in perspective when you write précis of these speeches.

THE QUESTION OF STYLE

The overall tone of the original should be conveyed in the précis as far as possible. Nevertheless, a précis is usually written in more factual and less emotive language than the original—for example, as mentioned earlier in this chapter, figures of speech, such as the metaphor, are often reduced to a more neutral form. Summarizing involves a move from the specific to the general, from the figurative to the literal, and from the dilute to the concentrated—tendencies which are bound to modify the flavour of the original.

Overall, it is more important to convey an author's meaning accurately than to recreate his or her style. You should aim for clarity and coherence. You must remain objective; your role is that of a communicator rather than that of a creative writer.

USING TERMINOLOGY FROM THE ORIGINAL

In a précis, you can use certain key words and expressions that appear in the original; it would be futile and dangerous to attempt to find synonyms for all the important terms the author has used. Peter Newmark writes, "Contrary to the usual advice, all words or phrases representing important concepts, objects, people, etc., in the original must be reproduced . . . ."[3] For example, the sample précis given in Chapter 3 of this book contains a number of terms taken from the original, including "fifth-century monk," "stone relics," "messenger stone," "millstone," and "ancient Chinese origin." Similarly, in the summary of the paragraph given in the first section of this chapter, the key terms "through traffic" and "local traffic" are used.

But using certain select terms taken from the original must not be confused with copying parts of the original that could be accurately reworded. The précis should not be a cut-and-paste affair made up of extracts; the emphasis is on re-creating the text in your own words.

ADHERING TO A PRESCRIBED LENGTH

The length of the précis is prescribed in the instructions, yet some deviation from the exact length indicated must be expected and tolerated. Many teachers allow a leeway of 10 per cent.

The length of the original should be indicated at the beginning or end of the text you are summarizing, and similarly you should indicate the number of words in your précis.

This raises the rather mundane question of how to count the words. My technique is to count as a word every typographically distinct unit that is preceded and followed by a blank space; thus any expression containing a hyphen or an apostrophe would count as one word. In other words, if you were to count all of the blank spaces between words in a text and add one, you would have the final word count.

---

1. Marcel Boret and Jean Peyrot, *Le résumé de texte* (Paris: Chotard et associés, 1969), p. 41.
2. A. J. Thomson and A. V. Martinet, *A Practical English Grammar* (Oxford: Oxford University Press, 1982), pp. 258-279.
3. Peter Newmark, "In Defence of the Précis," in *The Use of English*, No. 25/3, Spring 1974, p. 227.

Evaluating the Précis: Guidelines for the Teacher

Several separate elements must be considered when a précis is being evaluated and marked. First, and most important, is the *content* of the précis (including the selection and organization of ideas and the accuracy and clarity with which the information is conveyed); this aspect reflects the quality of the student's thought. Second, the student's or candidate's writing ability must be evaluated—consideration must be given to mastery of the mechanics of writing (correctness of grammar, spelling, punctuation, and so forth) and writing style (including factors such as the flow of the text, vocabulary choice, and readability).

When attributing a grade to a précis, the marker must consider each of these elements and base the grade on a combination of these factors. These separate factors can be weighted in a variety of ways. In *Le résumé de texte*, Boret and Peyrot mention one official marking scheme (used in several French schools of higher learning) in which 50 per cent of the mark is based on content, 25 per cent on mechanics, and 25 per cent on style.[1]

When correcting a précis that is to be returned to a student, the teacher must be sure not only to point out errors, but also to identify the *type* of error that has been made. It does a student little good to be told simply that something is "wrong"; he or she must understand why it is wrong and how it can be corrected. For this purpose, the teacher should use a clear marking system which identifies types of errors. The following is a sample system of correction symbols that can be used in the margins of a text to facilitate error identification.

CORRECTION SYMBOLS

Errors of Content

DISTORT	distortion of meaning
OMISSION	idea that should be included has been omitted
SUPERFL	superfluous material has been included
OVEREMP	too much emphasis placed on an idea
UNDEREMP	insufficient emphasis placed on an idea
UNCLEAR	lack of clarity
LOGIC?	error of logic
AMB	ambiguity
FACT	error of fact
INCOH	lack of coherence

Errors of Style and Usage

W	poor word choice
AWK	awkward construction
W.O.	wrong word order
C	colloquial
REP	repetitious
RED	redundant
JARG	jargon
SHIFT	shift in perspective; inconsistency
ID	non-idiomatic usage

CON	inappropriate connotation	/	(in text) lower case should be used
		CAP	(in margin) capital letter should be used
			(underlined in text) capitalize

Grammatical and Mechanical Errors

G	general error of grammar	≡	
V	incorrect verb tense or verb form	P	(in margin) error of punctuation
AG	lack of agreement	ℐ	(in text) omit punctuation
SS	faulty sentence structure		
ANT	antecedent error	∧	(in text) something missing
LLISM	lack of parallelism		
N	error of number	◡	(in text) join letters
PREP	wrong preposition	- - - -	(underlined in text) leave as originally written
DANG	dangling modifier		
RUN-ON	run-on sentence		
SP	error of spelling		
¶	start new paragraph		
LC	(in margin) lower case should be used		

---

1. Boret and Peyrot, *Le résumé de texte*, p. 17.

A Proposed Writing Skills Program for Translators

Writing skills courses can be offered at a variety of levels throughout a university undergraduate program in translation. In a three-year translation program, the writing skills component could be as follows:

Level 1

Content: Grammar
Vocabulary expansion
Composition
Error correction
Standard business writing
Paraphrasing

Before students can master advanced composition, translation, or précis-writing, they must have a good grasp of basic grammar. This level of training would include a review of parts of speech, sentence structures, grammar, and principles governing the mechanics of correct writing. A good grammar book would be used as the basic reference work. Exercises in composition would be included, with emphasis on coherence, consistency, and clarity in the structuring of the sentence, paragraph, and text. Standard business writing would include the business letter and curriculum vitae.

Level 2

Content: Advanced composition
Intralingual précis-writing

Interlingual précis-writing
Revision and proofreading

Advanced composition would include the study of specific types of writing (such as journalistic, administrative, and persuasive). Précis-writing would involve exercises in analysing patterns of meaning in source texts and drawing up finished précis. Revision would include improving the structure of passages, polishing texts, and rewriting jargon.

Level 3

Content: Advanced précis-writing
Summary-record writing ("oral" précis-writing)
Technical writing
Abstracting
Synthesizing

Students would précis lengthy articles or even entire books. For summary-record writing, they could attend specific extra-curricular meetings, lectures or speeches and submit written summaries of these; or the instructor could read speeches aloud to the class and have them submit summaries. The course would include a study of technical writing and abstracting. Students would also be required to write a synthesis-summary of related texts.

Bibliography

American National Standards Institute, Inc. *American National Standard for Writing Abstracts*. New York: American National Standards Institute, 1979.

Bongartz, Joseph. *Summary and Précis Writing*. Paris: Collection des études supérieures d'anglais, OCDL, 1970.

Bérard, Roger, and André Wilhelm. *Les méthodes de la dissertation, du résumé de texte, de l'exposé oral*. Paris: Dunod, 1971.

Boret, Marcel, and Jean Peyrot. *Le résumé de texte*. Paris: Chotard et associés, 1969.

Borko, Harold, and Charles Bernier. *Abstracting Concepts and Methods*. New York: Academic Press, 1975.

Chaumier, Jacques. *L'analyse documentaire*. Paris: Entreprise moderne d'Édition, 1977.

Coles Editorial Board. *Dictionary of Literary Terms*. Toronto: Coles, 1974.

Collison, Robert. *Abstracts and Abstracting Services*. Santa Barbara: American Bibliographical Center, 1971.

Cremmins, Edward. *The Art of Abstracting*. Philadelphia: ISI Press, 1982.

Delisle, Jean. *L'analyse du discours comme méthode de traduction*. Cahiers de traductologie No. 2. Ottawa: University of Ottawa Press, 1980.

Gallimard, Pol, and Claude Launay. *Le résumé de texte*. Paris: Hatier, 1979.

Gicquel, Bernard. *L'explication de textes et la dissertation*. Paris: Presses Universitaires de France, 1979.

Jackson, T. C., and John Briggs. *A Text-book of Précis-Writing*. London: University Tutorial Press, 1906.

Jepson, R. W. *A New Guide to Précis-Writing*. London: Longmans, Green, 1946.

Koberski, E. "A Contribution to the Training of Translators: Précis-Writing in the First Year English Syllabus Explored." In *Vingt ans d'enseignement et de recherche en traduction et en interprétation de conférence*. Mons: Université de Mons, Hainaut, 1983, pp. 177-180.

Markstein, Linda, and Louise Hirasawa. *Expanding Reading Skills, Advanced*. Rowley, Mass.: Newbury House Publishers, 1977.

Moreau, Jean A. *La contraction et la synthèse de textes*. Paris: Éditions Fernand Nathan, 1977.

Mossop, Brian. "The Translator as Rapporteur: A Concept for Training and Self-improvement." In *Meta*. Vol. 28, No. 3. September 1983, pp. 244-278.

Newmark, Peter. *Approaches to Translation*. Oxford: Pergamon Press, 1981.

Newmark, Peter. "In Defence of the Précis." In *The Use of English*. No. 25/3, Spring 1974, pp. 226, 227, 238.

Petroff, André. "Méthodologie de la contraction de texte." In *Langue Française*. No. 26. Paris: Larousse, May 1974, pp. 41-55.

Popovič, Anton. *Dictionary for the Analysis of Literary Translation*. Edmonton: University of Alberta, 1976.

Queneau, Raymond. *Exercices de style*. Paris: Gallimard, 1947.

Queneau, Raymond. *Exercises in Style*. Translated by Barbara Wright. New York: New Directions, 1979.

Roberts, Roda P. "Context in Translation." In *Actes du 10e Colloque de l'ACLA*, May 1979, pp. 117-132.

Rozan, Jean-François. *La prise de notes en interprétation consécutive*. Geneva: Librairie de l'Université Georg, 1965.

Russell, Pamela. "The Importance of Précis-Writing in a Translator Training Programme." In *L'enseignement de l'interprétation et de la traduction: de la théorie à la pédagogie*. Cahiers de traductologie No. 4. Ottawa: University of Ottawa Press, 1981.

Stalloni, Yves. *Méthode de contraction et de synthèse de textes*. Paris: Ellipses, 1981.

Thomson, A. J., and A. V. Martinet. *A Practical English Grammar*. Oxford: Oxford University Press, 1982.

Van Gorp, H. "La traduction littéraire parmi les autres métatextes." In *Literature and Translation*. Edited by James S. Holmes, José Lambert, and Raymond Van Den Broeck. Leuven, Belgium: Acco, 1978.

Vinay, J.-P., and J. Darbelnet. *Stylistique comparée du français et de l'anglais*. Montreal: Didier-Beauchemin, 1958.

Webster's New Twentieth Century Dictionary. New York: The World Publishing Co., 1974.

Witty, Frank J. "The Beginnings of Indexing and Abstracting: Some Notes Toward a History of Indexing in Antiquity and the Middle Ages." *The Indexer*, Vol. 8, No. 4, October 1973.

Part Two

Introduction to Part Two

Part Two of this manual contains a series of practical exercises in précis-writing which will give you the chance to put into practice some of the principles and techniques described in Part One. The exercises in Part Two follow a logical progression; Sections 1 to 5 take you from the initial stages of reading and comprehension, through analysing meaning, writing succinctly, and paraphrasing, to writing précis, first of short passages, and then of longer articles.

The last few sections contain more advanced exercises. The exercises in Section 6 require you to summarize spoken texts, a process which involves adapting direct speech to indirect speech. In Section 7, you must write English précis of French texts; these interlingual exercises are designed specifically for translation students and second-language students. Section 8 contains exercises on popularizing and summarizing specialized texts, and Section 9, an exercise on abstracting.

The exercises in Part Two are challenging enough to be used in college-level and undergraduate courses in English writing skills; many would also fit in well to an advanced course in English as a second language. Some exercises are more difficult than others; instructors can choose those which best suit the orientation of their courses and the abilities of their students.

Comprehension

The exercises in this section are designed to test your comprehension of expressions, sentences, paragraphs, and longer texts. In Exercises 1 and 2, you must explain the meaning of specific expressions. In Exercises 3 to 6, you must read paragraphs and then answer multiple choice questions on the tone, purpose and topic of each. In Exercise 7, you must describe the tone, purpose and topic of a number of paragraphs. Exercise 8 contains a longer text; you must answer general and specific questions on its content, and examine a sample précis of it for distortions.

Exercise 1 – Comprehension

Explain the following references.

1. the fourth estate
2. the fifth column
3. the Big Apple
4. a baker's dozen
5. a bleeding heart
6. Big Brother
7. Yes, Virginia, there is a Santa Claus.
8. Machiavellian tactics
9. to raise Cain
10. to bell the cat
11. to meet one's Waterloo
12. to have the Midas touch
13. his Achilles' heel
14. to be a good Samaritan
15. sour grapes
16. the Iron Lady
17. a Pyrrhic victory
18. Silicon Valley

Exercise 2 – Comprehension

Read the following sentences, paying particular attention to the expressions underlined. Then explain the meaning of each expression, as it is used in that particular context.

1. The company is offering a <u>state-of-the-art</u> career in the field of highly sophisticated electronics technology.
2. The union claims that the management has <u>ridden roughshod over</u> the workers.
3. The Member of Parliament for my riding is <u>a member of the shadow cabinet</u>.
4. Her cousin moved to the United States and is living in <u>a bedroom community</u> outside New York City.
5. The committee hearings were held <u>in camera</u>.
6. The company he used to run was a <u>fly-by-night</u> operation.
7. The article accuses the politician of <u>using laundered money</u> in his campaign.
8. The teacher of the computer course has a <u>hands-on</u> approach.
9. <u>McLuhan's global village</u> shrinks every year.

10. The candidate that I support has been trying to deal with issues at the <u>grass-roots</u> level.

11. The visiting dignitary was given <u>red-carpet treatment</u>.

12. My roommate had never wanted for anything; he <u>was born with a silver spoon in his mouth</u>.

13. The papermill employees have gone on <u>a wildcat strike</u>.

14. The politician explained that he had taken the money from <u>a slush fund</u>.

15. He will promise you anything and tell you exactly what he thinks you want to hear; be sure to <u>take his words with a grain of salt</u>.

16. After much discussion, they reached <u>a gentleman's agreement</u>.

17. When the accountant checked our books, he discovered that we <u>were operating in the red</u>.

18. The current government, like previous ones, is guilty of <u>pork-barrelling</u>.

Exercise 3 – Comprehension

Read the following paragraph.

> What needs to be said, emphatically, is that general university education—the BA and the BSc—is relevant and marketable. General education trains in thoroughness of inquiry, in skepticism toward pat answers and received wisdom, in the hard work of learning, in objectivity, in systematic analysis and in clarity and flexibility of thought, and these are not mere social graces but skills that are down-to-earth attributes of effectiveness in all vocations. Nor is the training that of the quick panacea immersions in Assertive Problem Solving or Executive Brainstorming that offer instant relief from normal spasms of intellectual insecurity, but an extended apprenticeship which transmutes these skills into powerfully influential attitudes of mind.
>
> James Jackson
> *The Ottawa Citizen*
> September 16, 1981, p. 6

Which of the following sentences best summarizes the preceding paragraph?

a. The prevailing attitude today is that a general university education teaches only social skills and has little marketable value.

b. A person with a university degree has a better chance of finding a job than does a person who has taken only immersion courses in problem solving or brainstorming.

c. A general university education is a real asset in all vocations, because it develops a wide range of intellectual skills and attitudes of mind.

d. Too many people today think that they can solve all their professional problems by taking immersion courses in Assertive Problem Solving or Executive Brainstorming.

What is the author's main intention in this paragraph?

a. to persuade people to go to university.

b. to reveal the superficial nature of the popular brainstorming and problem-solving immersion courses.

c. to show that a university education protects a person from attacks of intellectual insecurity.

d. to emphasize the relevance and value of a general university education.

Exercise 4 – Comprehension

Read the following paragraph.

> L.B.J. was, by all accounts, one of the most physically exuberant occupants of the Oval Office. He could sit a visitor down for a morning-long rundown on the intellectual capacity and personal habits of every member of the Senate. He had a grand way of picking his nose, scratching himself and eating food off other people's plates. When the pope had difficulty opening a present that Johnson handed him, L.B.J. whipped a jackknife from his pocket and cut the string. He hated knots, especially when tied with red tape. In his impatience to get things done, he browbeat and literally manhandled associates. Hubert Humphrey recalled having been kicked in the shins affectionately but painfully. The Texas hill-country rancher would prod men as well as cattle. Yet, said Humphrey, "Many people looked upon him as a heavy-handed man. That was not really true. He was sort of like a cowboy making love."
>
> *Time*
> August 18, 1980

Which of the following sentences best summarizes the preceding paragraph?

a. Although L.B.J. was notoriously heavy-handed and rough-mannered, many Americans loved him.

b. L.B.J. was a colourful, exuberant, rough-mannered, and physically forceful president with no time for formalities or red tape.

c. When L.B.J. occupied the Oval Office, he insulted and manhandled many people and acted in a manner unbecoming to a president.

d. Despite his rough-mannered ways, L.B.J. was well-informed about the activities of all the people who worked for him.

Which of the following selections best explains the author's main intention in this paragraph?

a. to paint a vivid picture of a colourful president.

b. to convince readers that under his rough exterior, L.B.J. was really a kind, considerate person.

c. to convince readers that L.B.J. was really an uncultured boor whose behaviour was unacceptable.

d. to explain why many people considered L.B.J. to be a heavy-handed man.

Exercise 5 – Comprehension

Read the following passage.

> More than most sciences, gerontology is haunted by primordial myths and fears: Faust sold his soul to the devil in exchange for a promise of immortality, and the Spanish explorer Ponce de Léon was shot down by native arrows in Florida while searching for the fountain of youth. But modern science has scotched hopes of physical immortality with the discovery that normal body cell lineages under optimal laboratory conditions will reproduce a maximum of approximately 120 times before dying out. Undismayed, gerontologists continue to track down the causes of senescence—the process of growing old—and possible means of extending longevity, keeping in mind that, as one researcher points out, "Death is as necessary a part of our existence as reproduction or breathing."
>
> Mark Czarnecki
> *Maclean's*
> February 25, 1980

Which of the following sentences best summarizes the preceding paragraph?

a. Throughout the centuries, man has tried to find the secret to immortality.

b. Scientists have discovered that there is a limit to the number of times body cells can reproduce: after reproducing approximately 120 times, they die out.

c. Gerontologists are continuing to seek the key to man's age-old dream of acquiring physical immortality.

d. Gerontologists realize that the inevitability of death precludes the realization of man's dream of immortality; however,

they continue to seek means of extending longevity.

Which of the following sentences is an accurate reflection of ideas expressed in the paragraph in question?

a. Gerontologists are haunted by primordial myths and fears.

b. The normal blood cell has a maximum life expectancy of approximately 120 years.

c. Gerontologists are striving to find the secret to immortality.

d. Gerontologists realize that death is inevitable.

Exercise 6 – Comprehension

Read the following paragraph.

> What then, is the present case? The supreme legislature of the whole British Empire has laid a duty (no matter for the present whether it has or has not a right to do so, it is sufficient that we conceive it has) . . . the people of America, at Boston particularly, resist that authority and oppose the execution of the law in a manner clearly treasonable upon the principles of every government upon earth. The mother country very unwilling to proceed to extremities passes laws (indisputably within its power) for the punishment of the most flagrant offenders, for the reformation of abuses, and for the prevention of the like enormities for the future. The question then is, whether these laws are to be submitted to: if the people of America say no, they say in effect that they will no longer be a part of the British Empire; they change the whole ground of the controversy; they no longer contend that Parliament has not a right to exact a particular provision, they say that it has no right to consider them at all as within its jurisdiction.
>
> *Dartmouth, in Great Britain*
> *at the time of*
> *the American Revolution*

Which of the following sentences best summarizes the preceding paragraph?

a. The recent treasonous behaviour of the American people is without doubt the first step in the total rejection of British authority.

b. If the American people reject the legislation that the British government has been forced to pass in the wake of American treason, they will be contending that Parliament does not have the right to pass this particular piece of legislation.

c. Great Britain conceives that it has the duty and the right to pass legislation designed to punish American treasonous behaviour and prevent further abuses of this type.

d. If the American people reject the legislation that the British government has been forced to pass in the wake of American treason, they will be in fact rejecting British dominion entirely.

Exercise 7 – Comprehension

Briefly describe the purpose and tone of each of the following paragraphs. (See page 13 for an explanation of what is meant by "purpose" and "tone".) Then state the theme of the paragraph in one sentence.

1. Precisely on schedule one day last week, controllers at Caltech's Jet Propulsion Laboratory in Pasadena, California, sent an electronic command leaping across 164 million miles of space. With that, Viking Orbiter 1, which has been faithfully circling Mars once every 47½ hours for the past four years, expelled its last puff of steering gas. No longer maneuverable, its electrical systems silenced, the unmanned spacecraft will now slowly sink until it finally crashes into Mars some time after the year 2019.

   Time
   August 18, 1980

2. Yes indeed, the 1980 Chevy Monza's got it all. Comfort and style, plus a way of making you feel excited about the prospect of driving from point A to point B. And at a figure that's not going to hamper your sense of practicality. Its sleek aerodynamic look invites you to hop right in and fire it up. But once inside, you'll notice standard features that are almost too good to be true. Like high-back bucket seats, a cushioned rimmed steering wheel, standard AM radio, a 4-cylinder engine, tinted glass, wall-to-wall carpeting, body side mouldings, bumper guards, hatchback convenience and believe it, even more. You've got to hand it to Chevrolet for figuring out how to get a sporty little car packed with all the things you want. And at a price we think will figure very nicely into your idea of what a sporty little car should cost.

   Advertisement for Chevy Monza

3. Technology means the systematic application of scientific or other organized knowledge to practical tasks. Its most important consequence, at least for the purpose of economics, is in forcing the division and subdivision of any such task into its component parts. Thus, and only thus, can organized knowledge be brought to bear on the production of an automobile as a whole or even on the manufacture of a body or chassis. It can only be applied if the task is so subdivided that it begins to be coterminous with some established area of scientific or engineering knowledge. Though metallurgical knowledge cannot be applied to the manufacture of the whole vehicle, it can be used in the design of the cooling system or machining of the crankshaft. While chemistry cannot be applied to the composition of the car as a whole, it can be used to decide on the composition of the finish or trim. . . . Nearly all of the consequences of technology, and much of the shape of modern industry, derive from this need to divide and subdivide tasks.

John Kenneth Galbraith
The New Industrial State
pp. 24-25

4. The way we see it, a few days of summer in The Bahamas can make winter seem weeks shorter. The sooner you start planning, the more time you'll have to think about soft white beaches instead of the next fall of snow! When you get here, you can trade your winter parka for a favourite swimsuit. And when you get back, you'll have a summer tan to remind you where you've been. Can you think of a better way to spend your income tax rebate?

   Advertisement of The Bahamas Tourist Office

5. Throughout the world, the threat to wildlife is growing from year to year if not from month to month. Wildlife is the victim of man's unprecedented proliferation; when animals are not being slaughtered, they are slowly but surely being eliminated through the destruction of their natural habitats. Many species are on the verge of extinction, either because their numbers have been drastically reduced, or because their natural environment has shrunk to a critical point, or, as is unfortunately most often the case, because both of these factors have combined to threaten their survival.

6. About Chicago itself there is so much to be said that the task of compression becomes hopeless. This is the most typically American of all cities. New York is bigger and more spectacular and can outmatch it in other superlatives, but New York is a "world" city, more European in some respects than American. Chicago has, as a matter of fact, proportionally just as many foreigners as New York, but its impact is overwhelmingly that of the United States, and it gives the sense that America and the Middle West are beating upon it from all sides.

John Gunther
Inside U.S.A., p. 395

Exercise 8 – Comprehension

Read the following passage, and then answer the accompanying questions.

Ecology is the science of the mutual relations of organisms with their environment and with one another. Only when we get it into our collective head that the basic problem confronting twentieth-century man is an ecological problem will our politics improve and become realistic. How does the human race propose to survive and, if possible, improve the lot and the intrinsic quality of its individual members? Do we propose to live on this planet in symbiotic harmony with our environment? Or, preferring to be wantonly stupid, shall we choose to live like murderous and suicidal parasites that kill their host and so destroy themselves?

Committing that sin of overweening bumptiousness which the Greeks called "hubris", we behave as though we were not members of earth's ecological community, <u>as though we were privileged and, in some sort, supernatural beings and could throw our weight around like gods.</u> But in fact we are, among other things, animals—emergent parts of the natural order. If our politicians were realists, they would think rather less about missiles and the problem of landing astronauts on the moon, rather more about hunger and <u>moral squalor</u> and the problem of enabling three billion men, women and children, who will soon be six billions, to lead a tolerably human existence without, in the process, ruining and befouling their planetary environment. . . .

Power politics in the context of nationalism raises problems that, except by war, are practically insoluble. The problems of ecology, on the other hand, <u>admit of a rational solution</u> and can be tackled without the arousal of those violent passions always associated with dogmatic ideology and nationalistic idolatry. There may be arguments about the best way of raising wheat in a cold climate or of reforesting a denuded mountain. But such arguments never lead to organized slaughter. Organized slaughter is the result of arguments about such questions as: Which is the best nation? The best religion? The best political theory? The best form of government? Why are other people so stupid and wicked? Why can't they see how good and intelligent *we* are? Why do they resist our beneficent efforts to bring them under control and <u>make them like ourselves</u>?

To questions of this kind the final answer has always been war. "War," said Clausewitz, "is not merely a political act but also a political instrument, a continuation of political relationships, <u>a carrying out of the same by other means.</u>" This was true enough in the eighteen-thirties, when Clausewitz published his famous treatise, and it continued to be true until 1945. Now, obviously, nuclear weapons, long-range rockets, nerve gases, bacterial aerosols, and the laser (that highly promising addition to the world's military arsenals) <u>have given the lie to Clausewitz.</u> All-out war with modern weapons is no longer a continuation of previous policy; it is a complete and irreversible break with previous policy.

Power politics, nationalism, and dogmatic ideology <u>are luxuries that the human race can no longer afford.</u> Nor, as a species, can we afford the luxury of ignoring man's ecological situation. By shifting our attention from the now completely irrelevant and anachronistic politics of nationalism and military power to the problems of the human species and the still inchoate politics of human ecology <u>we shall be killing two birds with one stone</u>—reducing the threat of sudden destruction by scientific war and at the same time reducing the threat of more gradual biological disaster.

Aldous Huxley
"The Politics of Ecology:
A Question of Survival"
570 words

1. What is Huxley's main purpose in this text?

2. Describe the style that Huxley uses in this article. (See page 13 for an explanation of what is meant by "style.")

3. Draw up a short list of key words or expressions used in the text.

4. Explain the meaning of the following terms:
   a. symbiotic
   b. wantonly
   c. overweening bumptiousness
   d. dogmatic
   e. idolatry
   f. treatise
   g. anachronistic
   h. inchoate

5. Paraphrase the ten expressions that are underlined in the text. You may make any necessary grammatical changes in the surrounding sentence structure to accommodate your paraphrase. See Section 4 for advice on paraphrasing.

6. Read the following précis of the text. To what extent does it accurately reflect the content, style and tone of the original? In what way does it distort Huxley's text?

Why in God's name does modern man insist on ignoring the relationship between himself and his environment? It seems to me he spends more time worrying about satisfying his greed and lust than thinking about how long our dear Mother Earth will hold out. Shouldn't we be concentrating on making this a cleaner, better place to live and not on trying to blow one another to Kingdom Come? This is a fragile community we live in, and we're all in the same boat together here on Spaceship Earth. We cannot afford to be foolhardy! We must not close our eyes to the decadence and decay surrounding us. Above all, we must not resort to violence. Let's put aside our political fanaticism and nationalism. Environmental problems can be solved with logic and reasoning. Let's lay down our guns! Wouldn't it be in our best interests to discuss clean air and plentiful food rather than running around shooting one another? And all because of political, religious, economic and philosophical differences? (How often we hear these excuses referred to as reasons!) We must turn in our swords for ploughshares. Let's all make human ecology our greatest concern. Let's avoid the death and destruction of war and reduce the threat of having nature turn on us as we have turned on her.

Adapted from a student's précis

Analysis of Meaning

It is important to be able to identify the major ideas and the underlying structure of a text. There are various types of exercises that can help develop this ability: for example, after reading a text, you can make a list of the key terms in the text, you can draw up an outline for the text, or you can identify ideas in the text as being either of primary or secondary importance.

The exercises in this section are designed to give you practice in analysing meaning. In Exercise 9, you must complete an outline of a text and distinguish between the primary and secondary ideas. In Exercise 10, you must answer questions concerning the pattern of ideas in a text.

Exercise 9 – Analysis of Meaning

Read the following passage.

Treasure off Tsushima

Almost 75 years have passed since Admiral Heihachiro Togo, in the climactic encounter of the Russo-Japanese war, sank 20 of the 38 czarist warships that participated in the battle of the Sea of Japan. The echoes still reverberate. Spurred anew by an old tale that Czar Nicholas II's sunken fleet had been carrying a fortune in gold and other precious metals, a team of divers six months ago reached the 8,524-ton Russian cruiser *Admiral Nakhimov*, in 314 ft. of water 5.5 miles off Tsushima Island, in an area between South Korea and Japan that lies well within Japanese territorial waters. They surfaced with a dull silver, footlong, 22-lb. ingot bearing Cyrillic markings. Said Salvage Chief Katsumi Uchinai as he displayed the bar before a packed Tokyo press conference: "At long last we have uncovered the treasure."

The salvage team insisted that the bar was platinum, but too "sacred" to be submitted to analysis. Some experts thought that it was too light for platinum and might be sterling silver. But after 15 more ingots were recovered last month, the discovery touched off shock waves almost as strong as those of the original battle. The find started a gold rush—to the delight of Sadami Umeno, mayor of Tsushima's isolated principal town of Kamitsushima (pop. 7,300). "We would like to have a hospital and a 3,000-ton ferryboat," said the mayor, suggesting that the treasure hunt entitled the island to some benefits it was previously promised. "We might even have an airport built."

Meanwhile, a Soviet diplomat called at the Foreign Office in Tokyo and claimed for Moscow whatever treasure was found; his stand was backed by Kyushu University's Hideo Takabayashi, a professor of international law. Abandoned warships, said Takabayashi, unlike abandoned merchantmen, continue to belong to the governments whose flag they once flew. Not so, said the Japanese Foreign Office. The find, it held, belonged to neither the Soviet nor the Japanese government.

That view sat well with Ryoichi Sasakawa, 81, famous in Japan as a philanthropist and longtime prewar supporter of conservative causes, an accused war criminal who spent three years in jail after World War II, and a multimillionaire whose fortune was made by, among other things, staging hydroplane races on which eager Japanese bettors could wager. Sasakawa disclosed that he had sponsored the salvage ship *Teno* and its team of divers at a cost of $13.6 million. The ingots and whatever else was found were his, said Sasakawa, who estimated that treasure worth no less than $36 billion was aboard the *Admiral Nakhimov*.

With that, Sasakawa unveiled a patriotic proposal: he would surrender the entire treasure to the Soviet Union in exchange for a group of islands off Hokkaido that the Soviets seized from

Japan after World War II and have steadfastly refused to return. Promised Sasakawa, with a chuckle: "I'm ready to talk with whomever Brezhnev-san might send over to my office."

Time
October 20, 1980

Now complete the following outline showing the development of the text *Treasure off Tsushima.*

Topic

Situation

Historical background:

Present situation:

Position held

by the Soviet Union:

by the Japanese Foreign Office:

by Ryoichi Sasakawa:

Below is a list of ideas taken from the text. Classify them as either primary or secondary in importance within the passage.

1. Nearly 75 years ago, Admiral Heihachiro Togo sank 20 of 38 czarist warships.

2. A fleet of Russian warships, purported to have been carrying a fortune on board, was sunk in the Sea of Japan during the Russo-Japanese war.

3. The sunken *Admiral Nakhimov*, a 8,524-ton Russian cruiser, lies in 314 feet of water.

4. The sunken *Admiral Nakhimov* lies off Tsushima Island, well within Japanese territorial waters.

5. Sadami Umeno is the mayor of the principal town of Kamitsushima, which has a population of 7,300.

6. The recovery of ingots from the *Admiral Nakhimov* has touched off a treasure hunt.

7. The mayor of Kamitsushima wants the town to have a hospital and a 3,000-ton ferry-boat.

8. A Soviet diplomat called at the Foreign Office in Tokyo.

9. A Soviet diplomat has claimed that whatever treasure is found belongs to Moscow.

10. Ryoichi Sasakawa was an accused war criminal following World War II.

11. Ryoichi Sasakawa made his fortune staging hydroplane races on which the Japanese could bet.

12. Ryoichi Sasakawa, a Japanese multimillionaire, is sponsoring a salvage ship and claiming rights to the sunken treasure.

13. After World War II, the Soviets seized from Japan a group of islands located off Hokkaido.

14. Ryoichi Sasakawa has offered to exchange the treasure for a group of islands that the Soviets had seized from Japan.

Exercise 10 – Analysis of Meaning

Read the following passage, and then answer the questions that follow.

The study of language and languages has been described as fundamentally democratic, in contrast with the study of literature, which is essentially aristocratic. Literature reflects human activity as carried on by the best minds, the intellectual elite of the human community. This description is not at all invalidated by pointing to anonymous or so-called "popular" literature. The mere fact that we do not know the name of the author of a literary work does not mean that he was not an individual, and that he did not elaborate, by his own intellectual power, his own masterpiece. "Folk" literature, in the sense that the entire population of a given community collaborated in its production, is a figment of the imagination. At the most, it may be said that an author gathered and expressed the inarticulate thoughts of those around him. But he gave those thoughts his own indelible imprint, and a literary author goes almost as often against the current of his environment as with it.

Language, on the other hand, is something to which everybody contributes by the mere fact that he speaks it. Parents transmit their language peculiarities to their children, teachers to their students, leaders to their followers, members of a social group to one another. Everybody lays his stone in building up the monument that is language. The contribution of the individual, anonymous member of the masses is occasionally a conscious one, far more often unconscious. The most fertile field for the cooperation of the entire community is language, which everyone, with practically no exception, possesses and uses. Therefore the study of language is a social science to the highest degree. Language is the tool and product of all human society.

Mario Pei
The Story of Language
283 words

1. What is the theme of this passage? Is there an explicit topic sentence?

2. How has Pei developed the theme? What is the relationship between the first paragraph and the second paragraph?

3. Find an example of a series followed by a generalization. Paraphrase the generalization.

4. Underline all the connectives in the text, and examine how they are used to establish coherence.

5. Draw up an outline for this text.

Brevity

There are a number of ways to achieve brevity in writing. You can sometimes shorten a text with virtually no loss of meaning by simply writing more concisely—by replacing an entire wordy expression with one carefully chosen word, by substituting a succinct syntactic structure for a cumbersome one, by eliminating repetitions and redundancies, or by recasting an entire sentence in briefer form. See *Methods of Shortening* in Chapter 4, Part One, for suggestions and examples of how to shorten specific sentence structures.

Another method of achieving brevity is to generalize—to substitute generic, or superordinate, terms for a series of words. This is the technique you must use in Exercise 16, in which you are required to find general terms to summarize a sequence of words.

As you do the exercises in this section, you will have the opportunity to use a variety of techniques for shortening texts.

Exercise 11 – Brevity Through Vocabulary Choice

Replace each of the underlined expressions with a strong, emphatic adjective. For example, "a <u>very stimulating</u> experience" – "exhilarating."

1. a <u>very nice</u> party
2. a <u>very bad</u> mistake
3. a <u>very detailed</u> analysis
4. a <u>very bad</u> meal
5. a <u>very poor</u> policy
6. a <u>very interesting</u> lecture
7. a <u>very difficult</u> problem
8. <u>very bad</u> manners
9. <u>very bad</u> pain
10. a <u>very important</u> decision
11. a <u>very heavy</u> rainfall
12. a <u>very short</u> delay
13. a <u>very intelligent</u> student
14. a <u>very boring</u> speech
15. a <u>very strict</u> parent
16. a <u>very ugly</u> hat
17. a <u>very fair</u> assessment
18. <u>very luxurious</u> surroundings

Exercise 12 – Brevity Through Vocabulary Choice

In each of the following sentences, replace the underlined expression with a single word. For example, "The <u>legal order restricting shipping</u> was placed on certain vessels at the beginning of the war" – "embargo."

1. After graduating from university, they both found jobs as <u>people who calculate risks, rates and premiums for an insurance company</u>.
2. The bored personnel officer gave the applicant's résumé a glance that was <u>indifferent and done merely for the sake of getting rid of the duty</u>.
3. They were shocked; they found his comments to be <u>irreverent and disrespectful towards things sacred</u>.

4. The saleswoman who served her was <u>excessively submissive and servile</u>.

5. After he resigned from the company, it was taken over by a <u>combination of business interests that agree to regulate prices and production to obtain maximum profits</u>.

6. He was tried and found guilty of <u>intentionally and maliciously setting fire to a building</u>.

7. His remarkable understanding of other people and their needs is <u>not based on reasoning or instruction</u>.

8. The leader of the new political movement is a <u>person who agitates so as to play on people's emotions and prejudices for personal power</u>.

9. He was a musical genius, and was only twenty-one when he wrote his first <u>musical composition for one or more solo instruments accompanied by an orchestra</u>.

10. The king travelled <u>with his name, identity and rank concealed</u> in order to avoid publicity.

11. After the rebellion was crushed, the president granted <u>a general pardon for past offences against the government</u> to all who had plotted against him.

12. Her brother, a <u>person who leads a secluded, solitary life</u>, lives in a small cabin in the Yukon.

13. Because his statement to the press was <u>capable of being interpreted in two or more possible ways</u>, the question remained unresolved.

Exercise 13 – Brevity Through Vocabulary Choice

In each of the following sentences, replace the underlined group of words with a single word which would convey the same meaning. This exercise is similar to the previous one.

1. She was an ideal employee: her conduct was <u>worth imitating and it served as a good model for everyone else</u>.

2. The jury acquitted the prisoner because the evidence against him was <u>not convincing or sufficient to decide the matter</u>.

3. Some people find that the climate in the tropics is <u>one which weakens them and makes them feeble</u>.

4. "Meat" and "meet" are <u>words having the same pronunciation but different meanings</u>.

5. He decided to devote his life to the church and became a <u>person who practices rigorous self-denial and self-discipline for religious reasons</u>.

6. She would be well-advised to <u>try to equal or surpass</u> the efforts of her colleague.

7. His father was a wise and thoughtful man, and he bore the trials of his life with <u>a calmness and serenity of mind</u>.

8. He clung to his political beliefs, and in any sort of debate he was <u>uncompromising and unwilling to agree or be reconciled</u>.

9. Before she left Russia, she had barely escaped being a victim of an <u>organized attack against a religious minority</u>.

10. Jason has a <u>natural inclination and aptitude</u> for all things mechanical.

11. Research has shown that, in an election, the <u>candidate who actually holds the office at that time</u> has the best chance of winning.

12. We felt that the reporter had <u>twisted</u> the story <u>out of shape</u> in his article.

13. The newspaper printed her statement <u>in exactly the same words she had used</u>.

14. In winter, the frosted windows on the old house are <u>capable of letting light through without being transparent</u>.

15. The fact that I was at the airport when his plane arrived was merely a <u>remarkable yet chance occurrence of two events at the same time</u>.

16. Dr. Maurice Henry, the newest member of the biology department, is a noted <u>person skilled in the branch of zoology that deals with birds</u>.

17. The police released him when they heard his <u>story which proved that he could not have been on the scene at the time the crime was committed</u>.

Exercise 14 – Brevity Through Rewriting

Remove redundant and nonessential words and structures from the following sentences. Rewrite the sentences if necessary. For example, "This article demonstrates the fact that the inevitable nature of class struggle cannot be avoided," can be rewritten as, "This article shows that class struggle is inevitable."

1. Northern Canada is large in magnitude and has a small, scattered population living over a vast area.

2. He was wearing socks that were of a purple colour.

3. To the seasoned traveller, India has a wide variety of adventures and experiences to offer him.

4. Water pollution, which is the most flagrant form of pollution, can be found in rivers, oceans, etc. just about everywhere in the entire world.

5. As for her father, it was obvious that he was feeling angry.

6. He was the first originator of a theory that is now unanimously accepted by all: that both genetics and environment have a determining influence on personality development.

7. There were only a few of the competitors that completed the race to the finish.

8. All students entering the Spanish program are required to take placement tests, which are designed for the purpose of determining the appropriate class level (beginner, intermediate, or advanced) that the student should be placed in.

9. Despite the genuine sincerity of his testimony, the accused was sentenced to three separate prison terms, to be served consecutively one after the other.

10. One of the objectives that a driver training course should aim for is to develop the student's self-confidence in his own abilities.

Exercise 15 – Brevity Through Rewriting

Rewrite the following sentences, expressing the same ideas in as few as words as possible. For example, "Specialists in the medical profession are delighted with the degree to which the new drug is effective and with the fact that the new drug can be sold at a low cost," could be rewritten as, "Doctors are delighted with the new drug's effectiveness and affordability."

1. He took courses that were offered in the summer in order to satisfy the requirements for obtaining a teacher's certificate.

2. It is up to all of the members of the public to assume the responsibility of ensuring that this type of occurrence does not happen again.

3. Eric George was a baker by trade, making bread in Montreal and then moving to Sherbrooke, where he continued to bake bread.

4. If we discover that the washing machine cannot be repaired, we shall then supply you with another washing machine.

5. As far as the average students are concerned, it is most likely that many of them are not actively involved in the politics of the student body.

6. The promising results of the experiments seemed all the more promising because no one had expected the experiments to turn out so well.

7. All ski equipment is expensive to buy, but when we compare the price of downhill ski equipment with the price of cross-country ski equipment, we can see that the former of the two is more expensive.

8. If you are applying for a job and you have experience but you do not speak a second language, then you run the risk of losing the chance of getting that job; the job might be given instead to someone who has no experience but who is bilingual, simply because that's what is required today.

9. In this job, my main task is to answer the phone, to photocopy material given to me by secretaries and other people, and to keep a record of everything that comes in and goes out of the office so that we will always know where everything is; moreover, my position requires me to supervise the operation of the mailroom in order to ensure that maximum efficiency is achieved.

10. The structure of the family today is quite different from the way it was in previous generations, the main difference being that today most families are made up of only the father, the mother, and the children, whereas in the past, grandparents, as well as grandchildren, uncles, aunts, and other assorted relatives were considered to be one family unit.

11. When we received Miss Jones' application for a position working as an employee of our firm, Miss Jones listed you as one of her former employers; would you kindly give us an assessment of your opinion of her abilities as a translator?

12. Some translators translate because they have a great deal of interest in their work and because they enjoy the actual experience of translating; other translators translate because the profession is a source of a good steady income that they want to earn.

13. Once a person has learned a second language, a third won't be as difficult for him to learn or to understand, especially if the languages are similar: for example, if somebody were to learn French as his second language, then he could easily learn Spanish, because for the most part these two languages are alike.

Exercise 16 – Brevity Through Generalizing

For each of the following groups of words, give the term that best summarizes the group. For example, "period, semicolon, question mark, comma, quotation mark" – "punctuation marks."

1. rhombus, square, rectangle
2. ounce, quart, barrel, gallon, pint, pound, ton
3. Baptist, Presbyterian, United Church
4. violin, cello, guitar, ukulele, zither, harp
5. U.S.S.R., Poland, East Germany, Czechoslovakia
6. indicative, imperative, subjunctive, conditional
7. Zeus, Pegasus, Achilles, Medusa, Neptune
8. iron, copper, lead, brass, nickel
9. metre, gram, ampere, litre, kelvin, degree Centigrade
10. UNESCO, WHO, World Bank
11. The Odyssey, The Aeneid, Paradise Lost
12. pediatrics, geriatrics, obstetrics, gynecology, psychiatry
13. Cenozoic, Mesozoic, Paleozoic, Proterozoic
14. noun, verb, preposition, conjunction, adjective
15. trumpets, flutes, clarinets, oboes, trombones
16. football, hockey, rugby, boxing
17. oak, cherry, maple, elm, walnut
18. coal, oil, gas, wood
19. dentists, doctors, engineers, architects
20. crayfish, lobster, shrimp, crab, prawn
21. French, Italian, Spanish, Portuguese, Romanian
22. grapefruit, lemons, limes, oranges
23. rat, mouse, squirrel, beaver, muskrat
24. cement blocks, lumber, bricks, plaster, stone
25. snakes, alligators, crocodiles, turtles
26. karate, judo, kung fu, jujitsu, kendo
27. cooking, vacuuming, ironing, cleaning, waxing floors
28. painting, drawing, pottery, sculpture, metalwork, embroidery
29. parsley, basil, tarragon, sage, savory
30. lion, dog, wolf, bear, panther, fox

Paraphrasing

A paraphrase is essentially a rewording of an original message: the content of the original passage is expressed in different words. There is usually no great difference between the length of the original text and the length of the paraphrase. The paraphrased text usually follows the original text quite closely; segments of text are replaced systematically. Most of the vocabulary and expressions used, other than key terms, should be different from those used in the original; changes in syntactic structure can be made as well.

Paraphrasing can be considered a type of intralingual translation. Jean Delisle compares paraphrasing to translation when he writes, "La traduction intralinguale et interlinguistique sont deux formes d'une même opération intellectuelle: les équivalences d'énoncés existent entre deux langues aussi bien que dans une même langue."[1]

Therefore, translation procedures such as those described by Vinay and Darbelnet[2] can be seen to apply to paraphrasing as well as to interlingual translation: transposition ("upon his arrival"/"when he arrives"), modulation ("the glass is half empty"/"the glass is half full"), equivalence ("dinner is served"/"come and get it"), and adaptation ("to be on the dole"/"to be collecting unemployment insurance") can be used when transferring meaning within one language as well as between languages.

Paraphrasing often comes into play in the translation process. For example, if a source text is unclear, the translator may well consult the author or a subject specialist and attempt to paraphrase parts of the source text in order to clarify meaning. Similarly, in polishing the target text, the translator may well attempt to paraphrase segments of text in order to come up with a better target language wording.

A remarkable and entertaining illustration of the possibilities of the paraphrase can be found in Raymond Queneau's *Exercices de style*,[3] and in its inspired translation by Barbara Wright, *Exercises in Style*.[4] In this book, Queneau, and in turn, Wright, imaginatively paraphrase one short mundane passage in dozens of different styles of language.

Two exercises in paraphrasing follow. Also, see Exercise 8 in Section 1 for an exercise in paraphrasing specific expressions within a text.

Exercise 17 – Paraphrasing

Paraphrase each of the following sentences.

1. People who drive when intoxicated are playing Russian roulette.
2. Until that year, the liberal thinkers had been effectively denied expression in the media.
3. In the new agreement, the union had given ground on several points.
4. When he became chairman of the commission, he found himself at the centre of a policy vacuum.

5. In order to have his proposal adopted, he had to pick his way carefully through the bureaucracy.

6. One reason that many universities and colleges will be able to live within their means this year is the unexpected surge in enrolment fuelled by the recession.

7. At that time, he was flying high with the success of his novel.

8. The representative that we are sending is a veteran of scores of conventions.

9. The fact that he asked his supporters to come forward is a measure of the fragility of his leadership.

10. Many Canadians have decided to pursue a higher education in the hope that improved qualifications will help them crack the job market.

Exercise 18 – Paraphrasing

Paraphrase each of the following paragraphs, replacing all but key expressions by terms of your own.

1. New technologies and consumer demands are altering our very perception of what is a salable commodity. Computer stores weren't even a dream in the 1960s. Information services weren't viable until recently, and who would have seriously thought there was a market for tanning clinics? Increasingly in this environment, we are coming to the realization that any commodity of value offered to the public is done so in some retail context.

The Futurist
December 1983, p. 17

2. Evidence has been mounting for some time that the prevalence and incidence of mental illness in the community are much greater than the treated rates because many cases are either not treated or are handled by others than psychiatrists, mental health clinics, and mental hospitals. This is apparently true even for quite serious forms of mental illness.

International Dictionary of the Social Sciences, ed. David L. Sills, Macmillan, p. 224

---

1. Jean Delisle, *L'analyse du discours comme méthode de traduction* (Ottawa: University of Ottawa Press, 1980), p. 204.
2. J.-P. Vinay and J. Darbelnet, *Stylistique comparée du français et de l'anglais* (Montreal: Didier-Beauchemin, 1958), pp. 50-54.
3. Raymond Queneau, *Exercices de style* (Paris: Gallimard, 1947).
4. Raymond Queneau, *Exercises in Style*, trans. Barbara Wright (New York: New Directions, 1979).

Précis-Writing

This section contains a selection of texts for you to précis. As you do the exercises, be methodical. Be sure to read each text carefully, taking note of any distinctive features of tone or style. Underline key terms; identify the topic of each paragraph. After you write your précis, count the number of words in it and see how close you are to the required length. Revise your draft carefully; it should be able to stand alone as a piece of composition. If you have any questions, consult Chapters 3 and 4 of Part One for guidelines on writing a précis.

The section begins with a sample précis. Exercises 19 to 22 consist of paragraphs and short texts to summarize. In Exercises 23 and 24, you must summarize letters, and in Exercise 25, instructions. The last few texts in this section are considerably longer and more challenging.

Sample Original Text

The Ivory Coast is a country awash with goods. The money comes from the land. There is no oil in the Ivory Coast (though promising offshore deposits have recently been discovered) and no major mining. But practically everything that can grow, does. The country is the world's third leading coffee exporter and has become first in cocoa (in part thanks to beans smuggled in from Ghana, its troubled eastern neighbor). The forests of the southwest and the modern port of San Pedro make it a principal supplier of timber to Europe. Most striking on a continent of single-crop economies, the Ivory Coast has successfully diversified its agriculture since it achieved independence in 1960. The drier northern part of the country now produces some sugar, and the region's red dirt roads are lined with dusty balls of cotton spilled from trucks headed for the coast. The southern part has become Africa's leading exporter of pineapples and bananas.

George H. Rosen
"The Ivory Coast"
The Atlantic Monthly, December 1979
156 words

Sample Précis

The Ivory Coast is prosperous, thanks to its fertile land. It has little mining or oil, but it has a diversified agricultural sector, unlike other African countries which rely on single crops. The Ivory Coast is a leading exporter of coffee, cocoa, timber, pineapples and bananas; even the drier north grows cotton and sugar.

54 words

Exercise 19 – Précis-Writing

Summarize the following paragraph in approximately 20 words.

Too frequently, lightning strikes spell disaster. Each year several hundred North Americans are killed by lightning, and others die in the fires that follow in the wake of electrical storms. Ten thousand forest fires and more than 30,000 building blazes are caused by lightning. Damages to property and loss of timber are estimated at more than 50 million dollars annually.

Janice McEwen
Harrowsmith, July-August 1977
60 words

Exercise 20 – Précis-Writing

Write a précis of the following text, reducing it to one-third of its original length.

When several billion birds leave North America each autumn, they find, on arriving in their wintering grounds of Central America and the Caribbean, that their forest habitats have been succumbing to the machete and the match. More than three-fifths of the forests have disappeared during the past 30 years, and at present rates of destruction, there will be virtually nothing left by the mid-1990s. Moreover, the adverse impact on migrant birds of this forest destruction is amplified several times over. Because one acre of tropical forest may supply winter habitat to birds from five to ten times as large an area in North America (due, among other reasons, to the disparate sizes of the two regions), the clearing of a patch of forest in, say, Mexico is equivalent to clearing many times as much forest in the north-eastern United States.

Dr. Norman Meyers
Manchester Guardian Weekly
January 6, 1985
140 words

Exercise 21 – Précis-Writing

Write a précis of the following text, reducing it to one-third of its original length.

There is little doubt that the country pedlar maintained an important niche in rural life, bringing news to the farmers, buying their dairy produce, and selling them food, drink and manufactured goods. The country pedlar flourished well into the twentieth century, to be displaced finally by mail order, catalogue selling and the country store. However, it is no longer possible to accept the traditional view that itinerant selling survived only among "a dispersed rural population . . . which was narrowly constrained by their farm locations", and that urban hawking and peddling declined in the forty years following Confederation. As in England, "the pedlar's trade developed into an urban rather than a rural occupation; in a sense, the pedlar followed his customers into the towns."

Hawking and peddling survived because in both rural and urban areas they continued to perform a useful retailing function. They flourished in the gaps left by other marketing agencies; they "fatten", lamented the *Canadian Grocer,* "on the neglects of the retailer." In the countryside they enabled farmers both to dispose of small quantities of dairy and other produce and to purchase basic necessities and small luxuries in a simple and convenient fashion. Indeed, small farmers living on the fringes of urban areas were themselves able to sell fruit, vegetables and dairy products direct to the consumer from door to door. Those living near Toronto, for example, were allowed to sell their produce in the city without obtaining a licence so long as they did not venture within six hundred yards of the market area. Those living on the outskirts of St. John's and Charlottetown continued to peddle milk and vegetables until well after the First World War.

John Benson
"Hawking and Peddling in Canada, 1897-1914"

Histoire sociale/Social History
Vol. XVIII, No. 35, May 1985
275 words

Exercise 22 – Précis-Writing

Write a précis of the following text, reducing it to one-third of its original length.

Privately-owned land is private property. It is protected by the law because it symbolizes individual rights, the right to benefit from developing it, the right to profit by selling it. However, this attitude cannot be maintained when there is a small minority of landholders and a large majority of landless people. In a situation of land scarcity, those with more land than they need cannot expect the government fully to protect their unused land against trespassers.

Squatters never occupy productively used land, even agricultural land. They occupy unused land held by private speculators or by government agencies. Squatters hold a traditional view of landownership - the ownership of use; that people have a right only to the land that they can and do use; that one actually establishes ownership through use.

What they lack is the legal tenure that will allow them to build for themselves, to develop their communities, and to obtain the required public services. Urban land reform which will provide the large amounts of land necessary for expanding low-income housing cannot be avoided. This is not likely to occur by government purchase of land in the open market. Zoning land for low-income housing, or creating laws for land expropriation are more realistic measures. Limiting the amount of land owned by anyone or nationalizing land are also important possibilities.

Shlomo Angel
"Seventeen Reasons Why the Squatter Problem Can't Be Solved"
The Southeast Asian Environment
218 words

Exercise 23 – Précis-Writing: Summarizing Correspondence

Summarize the content of the following letter in approximately 100 words.

Dear Board Member:

Some confusion appears to have arisen concerning our organization's policy on travel allowances for Board members who live in various parts of the country and must travel considerable distances to attend our Annual General Meetings.

Our policy for several years has been to reimburse Board members fifty per cent of their cost incurred in travelling to such meetings. At the Board meeting held on September 30, 1986, a decision was made to subsidize up to one hundred per cent of the cost of Board members travelling to the Annual General Meeting of this organization. This decision was not to become official until it was approved by the Executive Committee.

There was a discussion of the travel subsidy situation at a subsequent Executive meeting, but no decision was reached.

However, it appears that Mr. Donald Doyle, a member of the Executive Committee, in advance of the Annual General Meeting held on February 21, 1987, informed some Board members that they were entitled to a one hundred per cent travel rebate for their attendance at this meeting.

We regret that some of you may have incurred unexpected expenses because of this incorrect information. We were not aware that Mr. Doyle had promised this one hundred per cent rebate until after the February 21 meeting. Our Executive Committee considered the problem on March 3. Mr. Doyle's request that the one hundred per cent rebate be extended was turned down because it was felt that a retroactive financial commitment was unwise and unmanageable at this time.

Once again, we regret the conflicting messages you may have received on this matter.

Enclosed are the relevant minutes from the Board and Executive meetings where travel allowances were discussed last year. We suggest that all Board members think about the travel allowance system, and submit in writing any suggestions concerning changes they wish to see made.

Sincerely,

Chief Executive Officer

302 words

Exercise 24 – Précis-Writing: Summarizing Correspondence

Summarize the following letter in approximately 120 words.

Dear Professors:

The University Bookstore is at present undergoing complete reorganization. As you know, our aim is to supply students with the necessary books for their courses. In order to improve our service and at the same time to facilitate the taking of inventory, in future we would like to proceed in the following manner:

a. During February, you will receive a copy of the course list we had for last September, indicating the number of copies that we have left of each title. You will be asked to return this list indicating the titles you want us to keep for subsequent sessions. Please indicate at the same time any new titles you would like us to order for coming sessions.

b. On receipt of the list, we will proceed in the following manner:
• reserve the titles you want us to keep
• return to the publishers the titles you do not need
• order any new titles you require.

c. We will ask you to send us your course lists by the following dates:
• for the month of May: no later than February 15th
• for the month of July: no later than March 1st

• for the month of September: no later than March 31st
• for the month of January: no later than June 30th.

You may wonder why we are asking you to submit these lists such a long time before classes actually begin. Let us explain . . . .

a. As you know, we must process not only one order but several hundred orders. This task is very time consuming and takes more than one day to accomplish.

b. Obviously, we are not the only bookstore ordering books, and the publishers' policy is "first come, first served".

We can assure you that it will be to everyone's advantage if all make a sincere effort to respect this procedure. In the end everything will be the better for it; we will give you better service, your courses will run more smoothly, your students and you will be happier.

Your comments on this new procedure would be greatly appreciated to enable us to make the necessary corrections before its application.

Manager

P.S. Please send us your comments before January 27.

360 words

Exercise 25 – Précis-Writing

The following text consists of instructions for the maintenance of a tent. Write a précis of the instructions; your text should be one-third of the length of the original. Since this text is not well-organized, you will probably want to regroup ideas as you summarize.

Tent Tips

1. All tents are subject to capillary leakage. Avoid rubbing against inside of tent during rainstorm. Also, some rub-off is unavoidable if clothing comes in contact with treated canvas.

2. Always dry tent out before rolling up to avoid mildew. Never roll tent up wet. Also, dry poles off before storing. Wet steel poles left assembled will corrode.

3. Cotton tents may shrink up to one inch per foot in use.

4. No cotton tent is absolutely water repellant under all conditions.

5. Set tent up before going camping if possible. We suggest you spray it lightly with garden hose to set material. Allow to dry thoroughly before striking.

6. INSECTICIDE: Avoid spraying insect repellant directly on canvas and screening. It removes the water repellant finish from these materials and may cause leakage where sprayed.

7. Particular care should be taken to ensure damage does not occur to the clear vinyl window of the tent. When folding away for storage, keep this window as free as possible of sharp bends or folds. Sharp objects such as sticks, tree branches or furniture inside tent should

be kept away as the vinyl will pierce quite readily.

8. The polyethylene floor should be free of all moisture before tent is rolled up and stored. Damp or wet canvas, if rolled and stored, will mildew and rot.

215 words

Exercise 26 – Précis-Writing

Write a précis of the following passage, reducing it to one-quarter of its original length.

No Exit for Entrance

Motorists pulling up to the Entrance General Store get their gas from gravity-fed pumps of a sort rarely seen outside of museums. The store interior, with its hardwood floors and ancient icebox, is another museum piece, but the traps hanging from the walls, the locally made moccasins and the health food nook are the daily currency of life in Entrance, a tiny Alberta community 15 km east of Jasper National Park. People there haul water from a spring and shiver in privies; many heat with wood, some go without electricity and telephones. For the 60 residents of Entrance, that's the town's charm and they want their life to continue at its turn-of-the-century pace. But, with the sale of the town last week, a 20th-century tourist resort is looming on the picture-postcard view.

Entrance, named because it is the "entrance to the Rockies," is an anomaly among Alberta towns. It has been privately owned since it began life in 1910 as a station stop for the Grand Trunk Railway. Theta Homes Ltd. of Edmonton bought the town in 1975 because it was "a beautiful piece of property with a good future," but Theta's own financial reverses saw Entrance put up for judicial sale last fall. The only offer—$277,000—was rejected by the court, but Torium Homes Ltd., an Edmonton area real estate company that had been eyeing the town for a couple of years, came through with a better offer—"somewhere between $500,000 and a million," says President Al Sonnichsen.

Sonnichsen is clearly itching to improve his acquisition. He figures Entrance people would want to keep the homes they rent but the houses have to be "upgraded" and septic systems installed. He expects the rest of the 204 acres that Torium bought will be subdivided into a color co-ordinated, chalet-type recreational housing development for Edmontonians now 30 km away. "I don't know yet how far we'll go with development," he says.

For Entrance residents, just about any recreational development will be too far. "Gramma" Angeline Desjarlais, 86, who was expelled from Jasper National Park 65 years ago and has since lived in Entrance, has already declared, "They'll have to carry me out kicking and screaming." Other residents have taken their case to Alberta Culture, asking for an historic site designation that would protect special buildings. Charlotte Hrenchuk, an area resident, is most concerned about saving the general store, which opened in 1927. But there's also history, she says, in the community hall, the boarding house, the store manager's original home and a trapper's cabin (the trapper having once taken after one of the store owners with a gun).

The store, says Hrenchuk, caters "to a way of life some people still live around here" just as Entrance, itself, does. "Everybody here could afford to live in Hinton if they wanted to," she says, referring to the nearest busy modern town. "But they want the life they have here where you can tan hides outside without complaints. Entrance offers a choice. You can heat with wood or propane, do without electricity or have a TV. It's a life you couldn't find anywhere else. I'd hate to see the place turn into another little resort."

Suzanne Zwarun
Maclean's
February 16, 1981
535 words

Exercise 27 – Précis-Writing

Write a précis of the following text, reducing it to approximately 200 words.

Rabbits Do It but They Never Mow the Roof

Take five concrete eggs, slice off the tops and replace them with skylights. Join the eggs together, bury them in the ground, clear away a view at one end and what have you got? Bill and Paula Lishman's dream home, scheduled to burrow its way into a hilltop near Port Perry, Ontario, this spring and become one of Canada's first completely underground homes.

From the surface it might look as if the Lishmans have gone "back to the earth" a little too far—whole wheat bread, wood stoves and free-range chickens okay, but actually living in the earth, underground . . . ? The negative connotations are overwhelming and almost universal, atavistic remnants of the good old days when a caveman's cave was his deathly cold, dark, wet castle. This reaction is the greatest barrier to public acceptance faced by the proponents of underground buildings. They claim, on the contrary, that with proper insulation and water-proofing a completely underground home is infinitely more comfortable than above-grade housing, mainly because the temperature extremes are not so great: earth has excellent heat-retentive qualities so that, 12 feet down, in Canada's southernmost regions, the average monthly temperature only ranges from 47°F in winter to 51°F in summer.

Going completely under is an increasingly common venture in the United States where it is estimated that more than 3,000 homes designed by architects such as Jay Swayze and Malcolm Wells have already been built. However, the trend in earth-sheltered housing is to find a south-facing hill, partially excavate a suitable site and use the fill to cover or "berm" the three non-southfacing sides and perhaps the roof (one of this design's many advantages is that the owners no longer paint their house, they just mow it). The south face is glassed in to trap as much heat from the winter sun as possible. The heat is then recircu-

52

lated at night (a "passive" solar heating system as opposed to "active" solar collector panels).

With all these benefits, why aren't commercial buildings going under too? The reluctance of business to move underground reflects consumer buying habits, since "going down" holds negative connotations which may be transferred to the goods on sale ("bargain basements," for example).

Businessmen also have long been aware that natural light prompts more consumer spending than artificial illumination, just a minor example of how important sunlight seems to be to man's well-being. It is perhaps this characteristic of the primeval cave more than any other—darkness and the fear it spawns—that makes people think twice about underground living. Wrongly so, cry thousands of naturally lit earth dwellers and visionaries like Bill Lishman. He believes the shape of the living space can exorcise the demons of fear: "It's the flat, oppressive ceilings, the square box effect with all those dark corners that do it," he explains. "Illumination from side windows doesn't completely dispel the darkness, but with a rounded ceiling and a large natural light source on top it's like living under the open sky—every part of the room is evenly lit."

The security of a warm enclosed space, the exhilarating feeling of blue sky overhead, a beautiful natural setting unsullied by incongruous man-made boxes—what could be more habitable? The question may become academic. The age of mass-produced above-ground private homes, which was made economically feasible by uncontrolled suburban development and cheap fossil fuels, is all but over. Highrises too have had their day. In the future struggle for energy and living space, the only way to end up on top may be to go down.

Mark Czarnecki
Maclean's
February 25, 1980
602 words

Exercise 28 – Précis-Writing

Write a précis of the following text, reducing it to one-fifth of its original length.

Divorced from a Generation

The dissolution of a marriage, in many cases, not only severs man from woman but cuts adrift child from parent. The casualties of that rupture have been grist for the mill of therapists and academics analysing the demise of the nuclear family. But it is only recently that professionals have considered the role of the neglected characters in the divorce drama—the grandparents. It is becoming increasingly difficult to recognize the new species of family tree. With changing intergenerational relationships, it's being whittled down; branches are pruned with divorce, new buds are spliced on with remarriage. Consequently, with no legal recourse, grandparents may find themselves amputated from grandchildren and then often artificially grafted to step-grandchildren with whom they share no genealogical roots or obligations.

Grandparents' rights may very well become a cause célèbre—in the courts, on the therapist's couch and in research circles. This April, in Toronto, the American Orthopsychiatric Association devoted an entire panel discussion to the intergenerational impact of divorce, at its annual meeting for mental health professionals. South of the border, the Stepfamily Association of America was launched nationally, late last year, to act as a support network and lobby for remarried couples, their children and older parents. And research studies, such as the Remarriage Project at the Clarke Institute of Psychiatry in Toronto, are examining the place grandparents hold in "reconstituted" families.

"There are few roles with less power than those of grandparents who are denied access or find the new relationship [with the remarried couple] less than cordial," says California psychologist and step-grandmother Emily Visher. Author of *Stepfamilies*, a guide for therapists, she says many grandparents find themselves at a loss in dealing with loyalties divided between their true- and step-grandchild. There is no prescribed social etiquette dictating how to handle such awkward matters as inheritances, gift giving and special outings, for example. More important, there is no prescribed legal status. Visher, who heads the Stepfamily Association of America, says it is only recently that American courts have begun to grant visiting rights to grandparents. (The precedent hasn't been set in Canada, but the demand may soon become apparent. According to the latest figures, one child in 10 now lives in a stepfamily.)

Not only have the courts ignored them, but most family specialists have not yet begun to appreciate the effect family discord has on the grandparents—and vice versa. "I feel very hurt now," says one Toronto woman about her relationship with her separated son's two daughters, 9 and 11. "They've become very discreet. They've been told never to talk about things outside the house. They're petrified." Reluctant to discuss family matters openly but drawn into the adversarial system despite themselves, grandparents often prejudice their grandchildren against the in-law parent, says Lillian Messinger, head of the Clarke Institute project. When disappointed with their offspring's new partner, grandparents may also use their grandchildren as pawns to disrupt the fledgling relationship. And in cases where the young child lives with his grandparent, the problem is further aggravated: not only does the divorce deal him a blow, but his parent's remarriage could result in a second loss—that of the grandparent-caretaker.

Separation or divorce has the potential of cementing ties between grandparents and their children or dissecting them completely. In one of Messinger's cases, a mother sided so entirely with her daughter-in-law following the divorce that she cut adrift her son, his new wife and stepchildren, and refuses even to see them.

Just as therapists for the most part, admits Messinger, have failed to include grandparents in family sessions, it is a general reflection of society's lack of respect for the extended family that grandparents are becoming more and more ostracized. "There are times when I'm left out completely," says one Toronto grandmother. "The behavior pattern seems to be if it's good I'll know about it. If it's bad I won't. They would like to protect me from the truth." Just how blatantly grandparents are ignored in divorce cases is no better illustrated than in the Oscar-winning film *Kramer vs. Kramer*, praised for its sensitive treatment of a ruptured relationship. The parents' anguish and a child's bruised psyche were parlayed into a box-office hit. But where, oh where, were the grandparents?

Toba Korenblum
Maclean's
June 2, 1980
708 words

Exercise 29 – Précis-Writing

Write a précis of the following text, reducing it to approximately 300 words.

Northern Canada

Northern Canada, or simply "the North", has many possible definitions—geographic, social, political, climatic, economic and so on; and it is not my intention to try to draw a rigid line between northern and southern Canada which satisfies all possible definitions. As a geographic region of Canada, the North is usually taken to mean the two Territories, plus the northern quarter or so of the western provinces, most of the land area of Ontario and Quebec on or near Hudson Bay, all of Labrador, and parts of northern Newfoundland.

In social terms, the North is most strongly identified as the region where the indigenous peoples predominate, or provide a significant proportion of the society. Population figures for such a region are difficult to find because census data is gathered on a provincial or territorial basis. It is known from the 1981 census that, in a total Canadian population of about 24.3 million, there were 45,741 people in the Northwest Territories and 23,153 in the Yukon. Together the two Territories cover an area of about 3.77 million square kilometres, which is more than a third of Canada's land mass.

The Inuit population in all of Canada is estimated to number 22,700, while people of native Indian descent (i.e., status and non-status Indians as well as Métis) number 600,000 to about 1.1 million. There are estimated to be about 16,000 Inuit and 19,450 Indians (status and non-status) in the Territories. In the Eastern Arctic, the Inuit are the largest population group, whereas, in the Western Arctic, non-native people are now in the majority. In the Yukon, non-native people outnumber native Indians by about four to one.

Languages create special difficulties in providing services for native people as a group in Canada. The Indians have about thirty distinct languages or dialects which are spoken today; about ten of these are in use in the Yukon and Northwest Territories. Most Inuit use one of the two main variants of the Inuktitut language, one in the Eastern Arctic and one in the Western Arctic. Many native people, whether they live in the North or in the rest of Canada, speak some English (a relatively small number speak French), but the degree of fluency in the "official languages" is often very limited. In general, young people are more likely to speak English than are the older people.

The northern region is so vast and so sparsely populated that to think of its having an economy of its own is to exaggerate its cohesion. However, certain economic characteristics are found in common across this wide expanse: principally an underdeveloped infrastructure of transportation links, financial and trading institutions and communications networks, along with a heavy dependence on resource extraction and export as a means of creating economic growth. In the Territories north of 60°, which are administered by the federal government, an additional economic factor is simply the overwhelming presence of the many federal government departments, agencies, and corporations, and their personnel. In essence, northern Canada is a region of economic hinterland which is dependent on metropolitan areas in southern Canada or outside Canada for its economic life. The metropolis-hinterland relationships of various regions of Canada have been observed and discussed for many years, of course, by Harold Innis and his followers, in their studies of the staple products of Canada. It would be fair to say that northern Canada is the region most dependent economically on external decisions, and its people are the least able to set their own priorities and goals upon the economic actions taken in their vicinity by corporations and government institutions.

The pressures from outside the North towards certain kinds of economic activity have been evident for centuries, most typically in the fur trade and its influences on the life-style of the aboriginal people. Thus, southern Canadian or foreign pressures for economic development of the North (or perhaps more correctly in the North) are not new. The current attention given to the economic value of natural gas and oil reserves in the Far North, and the ways and means of moving these resources to the south (Canada or the U.S.), is simply the most recent of a series of outside efforts to extract wealth from northern Canada. The economic benefits of such development for large corporations, and for the highly paid workers they send in to do the physical work, are easily seen. However, the benefits (economic or otherwise) for people living permanently in the North are less apparent. As such developments have taken place in specific locations, there have been concerns expressed, especially by native leaders, about the high social costs incurred by the local people—costs which cannot necessarily be compensated for by money or jobs (usually short-term and lower-paid anyway).

Perceiving northern Canada as an economic larder . . . is primarily an outsider's view of the region. Most people living in the North, especially native people (who are not interested in living elsewhere in Canada), tend to see it differently. This is not to suggest that the people in the North agree on their vision of northern Canada or on what should be the priorities for development there. Many differences of opinion exist both among various native organizations and between native people in different parts of the North. Furthermore, non-native people are not unanimous, the greatest difference probably being between people born and raised in the North and those who have taken a job there, most likely only for a few years.

Jean McNulty
"Satellite Broadcasting in Northern Canada"
Explorations in Canadian Economic History
906 words

Exercise 30 – Précis-Writing

Write a précis of the following text, reducing it to one-third of the original length.

PCBs: An Environmental Nightmare

To the public, polychlorinated biphenyls (PCBs) suggest an insidious invading poison which threatens our environment, our food and our health. In Canada, the dangers of these chemicals first caught the public's attention in 1985, when a transporter truck leaked PCBs onto the Trans-Canada Highway near Kenora, Ontario, contaminating several vehicles and long stretches of road surface.

The presence of toxic chemicals, including the deadly PCBs, in the environment is an issue with obvious implications for land planners, agriculturalists, environmentalists and everyone concerned with the condition of the land and the quality of the soil. Questions relating to the storage and disposal of such chemicals must be solved in ways that are acceptable to all interests, and planning decisions must take account of the "not-in-my-backyard" attitude prevalent in most Canadian communities. . . .

PCBs are synthetic chemical compounds consisting of chlorine, carbon and hydrogen. They were first manufactured for a variety of industrial and commercial uses in 1929. PCB mixtures are usually light-coloured liquids that feel like thick, oily molasses, although some compounds form sticky, yellow liquids or a brittle gum ranging in colour from amber to black.

The major use of the chemical has been as a dielectric fluid coolant and insulator for electrical capacitors and transformers. PCBs were also used as hydraulic and heat transfer fluids. Until the early 1970s, PCBs were used in some electrical appliances; as surface coating for carbonless copy paper, washable wall covering, and upholstery fabrics; as plasticizers in sealants, caulkings, synthetic resins, rubbers, paint pigments, waxes and asphalts; and as flame retardants in lubricating oils.

Sources and Dangers

Widespread contamination of the environment with PCBs was recognized in the last half of the 1960s by scientists searching for traces of another chlorinated hydrocarbon—DDT. By 1972, researchers and scientists had established that there was sufficient evidence to indicate clearly that the release of PCBs into the environment posed a potential hazard to the environment and human health. Approximately 635 million kilograms of PCBs were produced in North America before their manufacture was banned in 1977.

Before being recognized as a problem, PCBs probably entered the environment largely from the disposal of products such as carbonless copy paper, sealants, paints and waste oils. Now, the main sources of PCBs in the environment are incomplete incineration, landfill leachate, leaks in transformers and hydraulic and heat transfer systems, and accidental release. Once PCBs find their way into the environment, they can spread through the air. Traces of the chemical have been found in oceans, Arctic bears, rainfall and people throughout the world.

It is ironic that some of the properties that made PCBs desirable industrial chemicals were also the cause of their undesirable environmental effects. For example, it is their resistance to decomposition that has contributed to their widespread presence in the environment, including their existence in agricultural soils. Once in the environment, PCBs accumulate in various life forms and the contamination passes through the food chain into freshwater and marine plants, birds, fish and other animals and eventually, man.

In 1973, the evidence concerning the release of PCBs into the environment and their presence in the food chain led the Organization for Economic Cooperation and Development (OECD) to urge all member countries to limit PCBs to enclosed uses, and to develop control mechanisms to eliminate their release into the environment.

The health effects of PCBs have been studied in animal species and, to a limited extent, observed in human beings. In several animal species, reproductive processes and enzyme and immunity systems have been affected.

Cancers of the liver have also been observed in rats fed diets which contain large amounts of PCBs. In human beings, the known toxic effects of ingesting, inhaling or absorbing PCBs include chloracne, eye discharges, headaches, vomiting, fever and visual disturbances. However, no conclusive, direct relationship between cancer and human exposure has ever been made.

Option for Disposal

The federal and provincial governments are cooperating to deal with the problem of PCBs, and ultimately to achieve their elimination from the Canadian environment. Actions are focusing on the establishment of a national system of destruction facilities for PCBs and other hazardous wastes; the implementation of a uniform system for the transportation of hazardous wastes, including PCBs; the development of environmental quality objectives and national standards for PCBs and associated pollutants; the prevention of PCB spills; and greater exchange of information on hazardous wastes such as PCBs.

At present, there are no approved destruction facilities in Canada for high concentration PCBs. Since 1977, PCB wastes, including PCB-contaminated equipment, have been stored, awaiting the installation of suitable disposal facilities. Temporary storage sites include industry and utility locations, provincially approved central storage facilities, and sites operated by small enterprises.

Some provinces are moving to establish and operate disposal facilities for hazardous wastes, including PCBs. The most effective method of disposal of high concentration PCBs is through high temperature incineration or thermal destruction. For disposal of low concentration PCB liquids, high efficiency boilers can sometimes be used. Chemical treatment technologies to destroy PCBs are currently being introduced.

Residues from incineration and other decontaminated materials can be disposed of in landfills, although most OECD member countries do not consider landfilling an acceptable alternative for PCB disposal. Only the United States, in specific sites in areas with geological formations of extremely low permeability, and Germany, in a large salt mine, use this method of disposal.

Many destruction facilities can be made mobile. In Canada, transformer oils with low-level PCB contamination are disposed of by mobile chemical treatment units. The advantage of a mobile system is that the impact of extensive waste disposal on an individual community is reduced.

As PCB-filled transformers come to the end of their service life, they are being replaced either by dry-type transformers or by units filled with an approved dielectric fluid, such as silicone oils or transformer-grade mineral oil.

Environmental Laws

Over the years, legislation has been enacted at both the federal and provincial levels to control the chemicals entering and contaminating the environment. In all, 24 federal departments and agencies administer 57 environmental laws; another 100 different laws are administered by the provinces.

Recently, federal Environment Minister Tom McMillan outlined the provisions of a proposed new *Environmental Protection Act*, which focuses on managing toxic chemicals by prevention. The draft bill is the result of two years of consultation involving leaders in government, industry, labour, environmental groups and the consumer movement, and will be introduced in Parliament this spring.

"Through stiff jail sentences that the courts will be encouraged to enforce, corporate leaders will be held legally accountable for their acts and for acts of their agents," said Mr. McMillan in a speech to the Canadian Chemical Producers' Association in November 1986. In addition to jail sentences of up to five years, the law allows for fines of $1 million a day to be imposed on corporate officers found guilty of pollution offences. It also puts the onus on industry to prove that new chemicals are safe before being allowed on the market.

Land
Lands Directorate, Environment Canada
Vol. 8, No. 1, April 1987, pp. 8, 9.
1,166 words

Exercise 31 – Précis-Writing

Write a précis of the following text, reducing it to one-third of its original length.

Evidence from the Ocean Floor — Firming up Continental Drift

Freezing rain, gusts of wind . . . an exhilaratingly miserable February morning in Halifax. The roads and buildings of Dalhousie University are ice-varnished. Here, in an office whose walls are hung with maps of the world's oceans, photos of geologists clambering over crags, and research ships at sea, Jim Hall serves coffee to a drenched visitor. On the table there are several smooth cylinders of rock. These are drill cores: much of Hall's formidable energies have been concentrated on wresting samples such as these from the least accessible of all parts of the globe, the three-quarters of its surface that lies beneath the ocean.

In the 1950s, when Hall was a student, it was known that the ocean basins were deep depressions floored with heavy rock. That was about it. The only answers to questions such as why the oceanic crust differs from the continental crust or how the sea floors formed were conjectural. The reason: between geologist and geology there lay a daunting barrier—an ocean several kilometers deep.

Hall started out as a land geologist doing field work in his native Britain and in Africa, using magnetism to date young volcanic rocks by applying the new techniques of paleomagnetism. What caused him to be, as he puts it, "bitten by the bug of the ocean floor", was a revolution, an intoxicatingly exciting and almost literally earth-shaking one.

He and a whole generation of earth scientists learned during the early 1960s to see the planet in an entirely new way. Continents and oceans, once thought of as fixed, were seen to be riding on rigid slabs or plates that make up the Earth's outermost shell. Ponderously jostling one another, these mighty plates form the surface of our world. Where they diverge, the sea floor spreads and new crust is formed. The public has come to know of these new geological ideas under the name "continental drift".

Some of the most compelling evidence for the theory of global plate tectonics (i.e. the science of plate movement and structure) came from magnetic studies of the ocean floor. Research ships cruising on top of the globe's most awesome mountain chain, the 65,000 km long submarine range that winds through all the oceans, charted striking and anomalous magnetic patterns—long stripes of ocean floor alternately weaker or stronger in magnetic strength than expected. In 1963 two British geophysicists accounted convincingly for these puzzling stripes by showing that they would indeed be formed if the Mid-Oceanic Ridges were the seams between diverging plates and the birth places of new ocean floor.

Consider, for instance, the Mid-Atlantic Ridge. From here, at about 2 cm per year, the North American plate (on which Canada rides) moves away from the Eurasian plate; all along this ridge, as fissures gape in the spreading sea floor, lava rises. Sometimes these undersea eruptions rise above the waves; in 1963 the cook of a fishing boat saw the sea boil up as Surtsey, a new volcanic island, was born just off the shore of Iceland. As molten lava cools it is magnetized by the Earth's field; thus, frozen into ocean floor rock there is a record of compass readings from the past. Welded to the trailing edge of the departing plates, new rock begins its slow journey away from its birth place. Spread across the ocean floor, then, are fossil compass readings, magnetic patterns which map, in space, a temporal history of the Earth's varying, wobbling, flipping magnetic field.

In 1971, Jim Hall came to Canada to teach at Dalhousie University and to investigate the ocean floor. He sailed out of Halifax that year on board the research ship *Hudson*, seeking data with which to test the new ideas about sea floor spreading. But the Hudson's dredge can only skim small rock samples from the bottom of the sea and provides no way to pinpoint where these samples came from. To get hard facts, Hall learned on his first marine geology field trip, one has to drill.

A year later, Hall and his colleagues began drilling into ocean floor from the margin of the mid-Atlantic volcanic islands: Bermuda in 1972, and in the following year, San Miguel in the Azores (where, quite literally, they got into hot water: their borehole pierced a reservoir of geothermal steam which is now being harnessed for electric power). In 1974 he was on board the deep ocean drilling ship *Glomar Challenger* when, for the first time, its drill string probed downwards through 3 km of ocean, through a thin veneer of muddy sediments, and then some 600 m into basaltic ocean crust. In 1978 he and his co-workers set up a temporary field laboratory in Iceland, and there, all summer long they examined rock cores that were being recovered by a drill rig from Noranda, Quebec; the cores presented a continuous, vertical profile of 3.5 km of sea floor.

Drilling ever deeper, from ships and from shore, organizing ever larger scientific teams, raising funds for ever larger budgets, publishing extensively, Hall became a driving force in marine geology. Much has been learned from the efforts of Hall and of scientists from many countries whom he has helped organize into the International Crustal Research Drilling Group.

Looking at a typical rock core from the ocean floor one sees, at its top, a thin layer of sediments; under this come the pillow lavas, rounded, often purple shapes characteristic of lava cooled underwater; then the sheeted dykes—basalt frozen like so many playing cards in the fissures characteristic of a spreading sea floor; below, the greenish, coarse-grained gabbro, lava which never reached the surface but froze here at depth; and in the mysterious regions lying still deeper, the heavy rock of frozen magma chambers and of the mantle.

Hall and his scientific partners have become adept at reading the messages written in such cores and in numerous papers they have reported their surprising interpretations:
- The outpouring of lava that forms the ocean floor, for instance, is not continuous; major eruptions occur once every 10,000 years or so, each fed by lava from a distinct magma chamber.
- Drill cores tell of volcanoes fighting to rise above the waves only to sink again and again beneath the weight of accumulating lava.

- One of the biggest surprises—the oceanic crust has been tilted, rotated, and structurally distorted.
- And, though the fact of sea floor spreading has been well established, no source has yet been found for the strange magnetic stripes. Drills probing for details within an anomalously magnetized block of crust reveal not the uniformly magnetized rock expected but instead a magnetic jumble.

The ocean floor, in short, is far more complicated than the tidy picture sketched by plate tectonics theory a decade ago. "After years of drilling merrily away," says Hall, "we failed to find the simple patterns we were looking for."

Usually when Hall says "we" he is referring to his close friend and collaborator, Paul Robinson. They met on board the *Glomar Challenger*, found they both were bitten by the ocean floor bug, and have since productively melded their specialties: Hall is an expert on rock magnetism, Robinson on structure and geochemistry. Robinson has taken three years leave from the University of California to work alongside Hall.

For Hall and Robinson, their next scientific expedition to study the ocean floor is not over water, but on land—the island of Cyprus. With the help of almost $2 million from science funding agencies in other countries, from Canada's Natural Sciences and Engineering Research Council and the International Development Research Centre, Hall and Robinson, a Canadian drilling crew, and an international team of almost 100 earth scientists are now at work on the eastern Mediterranean island. They are recovering more than 4 km of drill core from a chunk of ocean floor which somehow, during the collision between the African and Eurasian plates, was thrown onto the island of Cyprus, where it is known as the Troodos mountains.

It is an ambitious project. The plan includes investigating what Robinson calls "the plumbing system" beneath an exhausted copper mine. Hot springs on the ocean floor become, when fossilized, the ore bodies such as Cyprus was famed for in antiquity (the words "Cyprus" and "copper" in fact, are synonymous) and many of those we mine today. Such studies may well lead to predictions of where ore occurs, and perhaps to new prospecting tools. It is probable that drilling below the Troodos range will also yield information on underground reserves of water, a precious commodity on semiarid Cyprus. As well, earth scientists from many Third World countries have been invited to attend eight-week-long training sessions in Cyprus, to learn about Canadian diamond drilling, ground-water exploration, and marine geology.

The overriding goal, of course, is to find more facts about the ocean floor, and with them as raw material, to attempt the feat that challenges all scientists—to add new ideas to our stock of truths.

Séan McCutcheon
Science Dimension, C.N.R.C.
Vol. 14, No. 4, 1982, pp. 4-8.
1,496 words

Summarizing Spoken Texts

A written summary of a speech, of proceedings, or of other spoken material is called a summary record. Read the section entitled *Reported Speech* in Part One, Chapter 4, for general guidelines on converting direct speech to indirect speech.

In abridging a speech, you must make several adaptations of format to convert direct speech to indirect speech.

Change of person

Although the speaker may refer to himself or herself in the first person (as "I" or "myself," for example), you will use the third person ("he" or "she," for example) in any such references. Even if the speaker does not specifically use a first-person pronoun, you should refer to him or her by name at the beginning of your summary, and you can repeat this reference at points throughout the text. Do not, however, repeat expressions such as "the speaker said" or "she said" at the beginning of each sentence; it should be evident from the outset that you are reporting someone else's words.

Change of tense

Verb tenses must be changed in the conversion from direct to indirect speech. When the speaker uses the present tense, you should use the past; when the speaker uses the past, you should use the past perfect; when the speaker uses the future, you should use the conditional. For example, "I am glad to be back in Canada," becomes, in indirect speech, "She said that she was glad to be back in Canada."

Change in reference to time and place

Adverbial references to time and place must also be adapted in the reporting of direct speech. For example, "Yesterday I invited the ambassador to join me here to discuss the conference that will take place next year," becomes, "The previous day, the speaker had invited the ambassador to join him there to discuss the conference that would take place the following year."

But the writing of a summary record involves summarizing the words of the speaker as well as reporting them in indirect speech. You must combine the change from direct to indirect speech with the summarizing process.

In some cases, you can use a verb such as "promised," "criticized," or "congratulated" to convey a speaker's meaning. For example, "I am delighted with the work done by this organization; the members have worked long and hard, and have been tireless in their efforts," can be reduced to "The speaker praised the efforts of the organization." Similarly, "I am constantly worrying about the poorer members of our society, the homeless, the single parents, the handicapped, and the unemployed," can be summarized by "Mrs. X expressed her concern for the needy." "As spokesman for the committee, I am pleased to inform you, Mr. Prime Minister, that, after weeks of deliberation, we on the committee have reached the following decisions . . . ," becomes, "Mr. Y

informed the Prime Minister that the committee had decided . . . . "

When summarizing proceedings, you are faced with a situation in which the speaker changes frequently. Every time the speaker changes, be sure to indicate who is speaking. As in summarizing a speech, use indirect speech to convey the major ideas expressed. If several speakers make similar brief interjections, you can sometimes consolidate the material with a sentence such as "Senators X, Y, and Z expressed their sympathy to Mrs. V on the death of her husband."

Various organizations publish instructional manuals for internal use describing the drafting of summaries of proceedings. For example, the Translation Division of the United Nations in New York puts out a document entitled *Instructions for Précis-Writers*, which sets down specific guidelines that their staff should follow when summarizing proceedings.

A sample summary is given below, along with the original speech. The sample is followed by several exercises consisting of speeches to be summarized.

Sample Original Speech

Pierre Elliot Trudeau's Saint Jean Baptiste Day Message delivered on June 24, 1983

On Saint Jean Baptiste Day, all French Canadians are invited to search their souls to rediscover how history and their indomitable will to live have shaped them.

In an age where assembly lines and mass media tend to standardize lifestyles and rob us of our identities, French Canadians need this opportunity to rediscover their roots and celebrate their distinct culture. For them, Saint Jean Baptiste Day is a reminder to be true to oneself and to one's origins.

This does not mean, however, closing oneself to others. On the contrary, self-confidence encourages openness, as is borne out by French Canada's refusal to withdraw into its shell at every major turn of its people's existence. Though of French descent, they chose to be part of the Canadian and North American adventure without renouncing either their language or their culture.

Saint Jean Baptiste Day thus affords an opportunity for other Canadians to look at their franco-phone compatriots in a new light; to appreciate more fully the immense spiritual richness of the land we have built together on North American soil, where people of all backgrounds come together.

I hope that French Canadians, in Quebec and in other provinces, will share this Saint Jean Baptiste Day with their fellow Canadians and derive new inspiration from it.

214 words

Sample Summary of Speech

Prime Minister Trudeau invited French Canadians to use Saint Jean Baptiste Day as an opportunity to reflect on their roots and rejoice in their distinctive culture. He congratulated them for not withdrawing into themselves but rather for being open and active participants in Canadian and North American culture while still remaining true to their origins. Canadians of all backgrounds should appreciate Canada's rich and diverse heritage and share in this celebration.

71 words

Exercise 32 – Summarizing Speeches

Summarize the following excerpt from a speech in approximately 80 words.

Excerpt from Statements made by Barbara McDougall, Minister of State (Privatization) and Minister Responsible for Regulatory Affairs, Government of Canada, 1987:

The question is often asked: Why privatize at all?

Reasons for privatization differ from country to country and province to province, but in Canada the federal government's commitment to privatization is rooted in the Canadian tradition of creatively—and successfully—mixing public initiative with private enterprise.

Both have their place. The issue is striking the proper balance between the two.

In earlier periods in our history, it has been necessary for Canada to put an emphasis on large government doing many things. Today, though, the private sector is recognized as being more appropriately the principal stimulant of economic growth and renewal.

In Canada's early years, state intervention was important—in fact, essential—in building the great canals that opened our country to commerce; in assisting in transcontinental transportation through the building of the CNR; even in developing our national broadcasting system. National medicare and income support programs also resulted from government interest and intervention for the common good.

Today, Canada has a developed and maturing social and economic infrastructure. The emphasis on state ownership and big government growth that continued into the 1980s has to be curtailed or two situations will worsen: government deficits, used to pay for increasing state intervention, will continue to rise uncontrollably; and the private sector, the engine of growth in the economy, will be constrained by unnecessary and unfair competition and pressures from the public sector.

230 words

Exercise 33 – Summarizing Speeches

In 600 words, summarize this speech made by the late Olof Palme, former Prime Minister of Sweden, to the General Assembly of the United Nations on its fortieth anniversary:

Let me at the outset convey the following message from the people of Sweden and their elected representatives to all assembled here.

We believe in the United Nations and we are committed to it. We are all aware of the problems of the Organization and can look back at both its failures and successes. But the experience of 40 years has not weakened our dedication to the purposes and principles laid down in the Charter. And, more important, we look at our world today and remain convinced that the United Nations is only at the beginning of its history.

Let us not make the United Nations the scapegoat for problems that reflect our own shortcomings. It is not the United Nations that has not lived up to us; it is we who have not lived up to the ideals of the United Nations. It is by improving ourselves and our policies that we can improve the United Nations.

The United Nations is contemporary with the atomic bomb. For 40 years it has been our common fate to live under the nuclear threat, under the risk of the total destruction of civilized life on earth. There is no more urgent task than to try to reduce, and ultimately eliminate, this risk. Negotiations have produced some concrete results, but by and large the nuclear arms race continues unabated. The main responsibility for halting and reversing this ominous process falls on the nuclear Powers themselves. However, as pointed out in the Delhi Declaration, during the last 40 years, almost imperceptibly, all nations and human beings have lost ultimate control over their own life and death.

Many countries are technically able to produce nuclear weapons. When they have decided to forgo this option, it has been in the knowledge that they would not increase their own security but decrease the security of all. Many of us have formally committed ourselves by acceding to the Treaty on the Non-Proliferation of Nuclear Weapons, which was brought about by the joint efforts of the two leading nuclear Powers. We are now entitled to demand that the nuclear Powers fulfil in the near future their part of the deal, that is, measures of real disarmament and, as a first step, a comprehensive test-ban treaty.

We also have to make it perfectly clear to the nuclear Powers that, although there were, at the time, no international rules prohibiting them from acquiring these awful weapons, they should certainly not consider themselves free to put them to use at their own discretion. The non-nuclear countries, which would also suffer death and destruction in the case of nuclear war, have a legitimate claim to make their voices heard and to discuss with the nuclear Powers ways and means of reducing the risk of the planet being blown up, be it by mistake or adventurous calculation.

Any use of nuclear weapons would be deeply reprehensible. One can speak of an international norm that is gradually gaining acceptance. The time has come to consider whether mankind should not begin to study in earnest how this utter moral reprobation can be translated into binding international agreements. We should consider the possibility of prohibiting the use of nuclear weapons, by international law, as part of a process leading to general and complete disarmament.

The United Nations offers a machinery for co-operation between the large and the many smaller States in the world. It offers every nation an opportunity to participate in the work for peace and a better future.

The veto has far too often prevented the Security Council from taking action. The cure does not lie in an abrogation of this rule, but in the creation of an international climate in which the leading Powers recognize the necessity, also in their own interests, of reducing tensions between themselves and of taking collective action against disturbances of the peace.

Much can be done within the Charter to strengthen the ability of the United Nations to maintain peace and prevent conflict. The Independent Commission on Disarmament and Security Issues has put forward some proposals. The Secretary-General has in his annual reports described several concrete ways to strengthen the United Nations, and he should have our full support in his admirable efforts to improve the Organization's functioning.

The Nordic countries have presented concrete proposals in this regard. The potential of the United Nations could be better used if actions were taken early to prevent conflicts. The Secretary-General should be given full co-operation by all members of the Security Council in creating a more active role for the Organization in this field. In this regard, the possibility of peace-keeping operations, not only to contain but also to prevent conflicts, should be considered.

The United Nations has financial problems. Let me say quite frankly that it is deeply disturbing that the United Nations should have to struggle year after year with these difficulties. The sums involved are small according to any yardstick. The United Nations system cannot possibly be a heavy financial burden to any country. Selective withholding of assessed contributions and refusal to participate in the financing of certain United Nations activities do not reflect an economic necessity but a political consideration on the part of some countries. Ideas have been put forward to reduce the maximum share of the assessed contributions that any one Member State is required to pay. A more even distribution of the assessed contributions would better reflect the fact that this Organization is the instrument of all nations and make it less dependent on contributions from any single Member State. In that case, the rest of us would have to shoulder a somewhat greater financial responsibility. Sweden, for its part, is ready to participate in discussions to explore these ideas.

Peace is, of course, the fundamental aim of the United Nations. We have come to recognize that peace is certainly more than the absence of military violence. It is also stability in relations between States, based on the observance of legal principles. One field where co-operation between States is absolutely necessary is the fight against terrorism in all its forms, these cruel slayings of innocent civilians.

The rule of law is of vital importance to peaceful international relations. In particular, this is strongly felt in the smaller countries. When the integrity and independence of one small country is violated, it often sends a vibration of anger and anxiety through the hearts and minds of the citizens in other small countries. For them, the rule of law and the observance of our common commitments under the Charter are seen as imperatives for a future in peace and security.

My own country has experienced serious violations of its territorial integrity. This has brought home to us the seriousness of breaches of international law.

Article 51 of the Charter entitles a Member State to act in self-defence if subjected to armed attack. Unfortunately, this provision has many times been twisted to justify all kinds of military action. Should we continue on this road, the prohibition of the use of force, which is basic to the United Nations system, will become a farce, and the law of the jungle will become legitimized. You may sympathize with the motives behind some of these actions. They may serve national security interests, as perceived by the different States. They may be caused by provocation from others and they may be very popular among the citizens and voters of the respective countries. But the fact remains that these acts break the rules of international law and infringe in some way or another upon the sovereignty and territorial integrity of other States.

In such situations, we must react and protest, in the interest of world peace and international law, but in the long run also in our own interests.

This is not a question of working against anyone's interests, of favouring one Power over another. It is simply a question of upholding certain rules and laws that are there for the benefit of all.

In our era of growing international interdependence we have to recognize that threats to peace frequently originate from conditions inside the countries. Misery, hunger, denial of basic human rights are the causes of political and social upheaval.

Many speakers at this session of the General Assembly have voiced their concern over the world debt crisis. I share this concern. We sense a growing rebellion among the debtor countries against what they perceive to be a lack of fairness in the international economic structure. Demands for internal adjustment efforts are testing the limits of political tolerance.

We cannot allow heavy debt burdens to tear at the fabric of society. Relations between the developed and the developing countries must always be based on the realities of economic and political interdependence. The solution of the debt crisis will be a test case of the possibilities for sensible co-operation between North and South.

Brutal violations of human rights occur in many countries, but in South Africa they are written into the very laws of the country. In this way the policy of *apartheid* is unique in all its moral abomination. *Apartheid* is doomed, as is South Africa's illegal occupation of Namibia. While fearing that it will end in a chaos of destruction and bloodshed for which the white régime will bear full responsibility, we should not abandon the hope that a peaceful transition to a non-racial democratic society may still be possible through dialogue and agreement. It is the duty of the outside world to assist this struggle for freedom, for instance, by applying sanctions.

We are witnessing massive migrations on an unprecedented scale between States and between continents. The reasons are many, among them hunger, war, natural disasters, persecution. The cultural clashes that are inevitable in this process have led in many countries to a renewal of chauvinism and racism. It is time we became more attentive to this particular danger. We are helped in this task by the rising anger, enthusiasm and readiness to act demonstrated by some people of the younger generations. It does honour to them, in this International Youth Year, that they have adopted the watchword "Don't touch my pal". There are many adults, in and out of Government, who would do well to listen and take notice.

For many people around the world the United Nations stands for something very concrete, a significant element in their personal everyday life.

A child in Africa learns to read in a school financed by the United Nations Educational, Scientific and Cultural Organization. A farmer in Asia receives a sack of seed labelled "FAO"— Food and Agriculture Organization of the United Nations—or "WFP"—World Food Programme. The United Nations Development Programme, with its technical projects, touches almost every developing country in the world. Refugees in all continents are protected by the activities of the United Nations High Commissioner for Refugees. Women fighting for equality and dignity are encouraged by discussions in United Nations forums such as the recent Nairobi Conference. Many civilians in many countries have felt more secure because of the presence of United Nations peace-keeping forces. If, as we sincerely hope, the initiative taken by the World Health Organization and the United Nations Children's Fund to immunize all children in the world against serious infectious diseases by 1990 is crowned with success, innumerable families will think of the United Nations as a benefactor.

Many of the people who have such direct experience of what the United Nations stands for may have scant knowledge of the intricacies of great-Power politics and the workings of the United Nations organs. But they instinctively feel that the United Nations is essential, in various ways, to their well-being, perhaps to their survival. It can be hoped that they will form, over time, a much needed United Nations constituency, that they will make their voices heard, claiming a say, demanding that power politics, high over their heads, do not jeopardize their lives.

But there is already a large United Nations constituency. It is all those people who believe in the United Nations as an idea. There are tendencies, in times of cynical power politics, to underestimate this idea. But it carries a strong moral force. All people who believe in international co-operation, in the peaceful solution of conflicts, in solidarity with others, make up this force.

There are groups and organizations in many countries that actively work for recognition of the imperative of peace. A fine example is the International Physicians for the Prevention of Nuclear War, which has won the Nobel Peace Prize. Its members, doctors all over the world, say that there is no cure for the effects of nuclear war; the only way is prevention.

The United Nations must be permitted to succeed, succeed in the efforts to promote peace and disarmament, succeed in preventing ecological catastrophe, succeed in the fight against hunger and deprivation. There is simply no alternative to international co-operation. Only through joint endeavours can we hope to move from common fear to common security.

2,045 words

Exercise 34 – Summarizing Proceedings

Summarize the following excerpt from committee proceedings in approximately 350 words. Use indirect speech.

Excerpt from the Minutes of Proceedings and Evidence of the Special Joint Committee of the Senate and of the House of Commons on Canada's International Relations on July 18, 1985:

Mr. Langdon: Sir, are you recognizing that the costs [of free trade with the United States] include not only economic costs of the kind the textile people talk about in terms of jobs and investment laws, but also the laws of policy freedom with respect to our economic decision-making?

Mr. Beigie: Just let me say that in a boxing match one participant agrees to give up the freedom to hit below the belt, provided that the other participant agrees to give up the freedom to hit below the belt. And the real question of trade-offs is whether what we get in terms of what the United States agrees not to do to us is commensurate with what we would agree not to do to the United States in some kind of formal rule-setting type of mechanism.

Mr. Langdon: With respect, though, the hits below the belt which the United States has identified in the context of many of the countervail decisions which the ITC has made have been key parts of what we consider to be quite legitimate and appropriate regional industrial policy or the provision of ILAP grants for restructuring purposes. So clearly it is possible that our policy freedom to take these kinds of initiatives could be significantly limited.

Mr. Hamel: I do not know whether we are on the same wave-length here but, with respect, they are already limited to a certain extent. We . . . are a sovereign nation, fine, but we cannot have our heads in the sand; we are living in a competitive world. You cannot make a lot of money taking in your own washing. We are a trading nation and a great percentage of our GNP is done through trade, and we have to re-spect other people's rules if we want to trade with them, and they have to respect ours.

In a comprehensive agreement, we would be setting out those rules in advance of starting to play the game, and I think that is a great advantage. Then we determine our policies in advance and know what they are. If people do not want to play our game, fine. If they do, then we play according to rules that are known in advance. . . .

The Joint Chairman (Mr. Hockin): Mr. Cyr, I notice that in your brief you did not call for free trade, that state of grace which is virtually so abstract that people do not understand. You called for a comprehensive trade agreement. To pursue Mr. Langdon's question in perhaps a different way, let us talk about policy freedom for a minute. What do you mean by a comprehensive trade agreement? Let me just list some things and ask you whether or not it could include some of these freedoms I might be concerned about.

First of all, could a comprehensive trade agreement include a transition period on tariffs and on export subsidies? Could it include protection for infant industries? Could it include the changing of duties when currency values change dramatically between the two countries? Could it leave realistic scope for government procurement? Could it include exceptions for cultural publishing and other industries in the cultural orbit? Could it include a beginning of discussions to lower barriers on services, but not an immediate state of grace of free trade on services? Would a comprehensive trade agreement still be, in your minds, a comprehensive trade agreement if it included things such as all those exceptions?

Mr. Cyr: . . . . I guess the answer is yes. What you are doing, in effect, is this. I assume Canada would put on the table a certain number of things it wants to do or protect or phase in or have transition mechanisms for, and the Americans will come in with certain other demands, and then we start discussing. I think it is very difficult at this stage for anyone to say the end result of a comprehensive trade agreement is, by definition, something we cannot agree with. We do not know what the end result will be, and as I said earlier, I do not think we would want to have a comprehensive trade agreement at any price. We may have different views individually as to the price we have to pay compared to the benefits we might derive, but it seems to me that in the overall scheme of things we will be negotiating a comprehensive agreement.

I think it would be closer to free trade than what we have today. If one takes free trade in the absolute sense that Canada is, in effect, California, which is about the size of market we represent, I do not think that is what we are talking about. We are talking about a comprehensive agreement that would obviously, over time, eliminate the tariff and lower the barriers and do a number of things, and provide access for Canadian goods to the US market. In return, we may have to change certain things . . .

The Joint Chairman (Mr. Hockin): Why do you think people keep referring to this discussion as a discussion of free trade when very few people who have come to us have even discussed free trade? They have discussed at most freer trade or a comprehensive trade agreement, but they have never used this almost intellectual abstraction, free trade, when they speak about liberalization.

Mr. Cyr: Carl, do you want to say something?

The Joint Chairman (Mr. Hockin): What do you think?

Mr. Beigie: I will be very blunt about this. I do not think anybody who has looked at this very seriously really thinks the notion of the idealistic end results of total free trade is what anybody is talking about in either Canada or the United States when they are in their right minds. There is no way, with people who have studied this over a long period of time, that you would get the necessary political support in Canada, particularly, for a notion that tomorrow we are going to wake up and there will be no barriers between the countries.

The Joint Chairman (Mr. Hockin): Mr. Beigie, let me just put this to you. In major newspapers across this country, the words "free trade" are in every headline. That straw-man abstraction is in every headline across the country. So somehow the press seems to feel it is necessary to use these two words, even though I agree with you we are not discussing them.

Mr. Beigie: In my experience, when you are dealing with a complicated political economy topic such as a comprehensive trade agreement, it is easier to go with a simpler concept, free trade. But I would argue vehemently that the people who are discussing this have more in their heads than the simplistic notion of the ultimate of free trade.

1,129 words

Interlingual Précis-Writing

When writing a précis in a language other than that of the original, you can follow the same approach as in intralingual précis-writing, but you must add an additional step: you must shift from one language to another. This shift can be made either at the outline stage, or later on, at the drafting stage. You may wish to draw up your outline in the target language, translating the main ideas as you analyse the meaning. You may, on the other hand, prefer to switch languages at a later stage: you may draw up your outline in the source language, and then shift to the target language when you start writing the draft.

A sample interlingual précis is given below; the original text is in French and the précis, in English. A sample analysis and an outline of the major themes are given for the text. Notice that they have been drawn up in English; the shift to the target language has been made at an early stage.

Sample Interlingual Précis-Source Text

Icare pour tous

Le mardi 12 juillet, quelque 120 « aviateurs » ont décollé pour le premier tour de France des U.l.m., les ultralégers motorisés. Cette nouvelle forme d'aviation populaire est dans le vent. La Fédération française des planeurs U.l.m. compte déjà 3 000 licenciés sur les 5 000 pratiquants recensés.

Cet engouement rappelle le boom de la planche à voile. Il est suffisant, en tout cas, pour susciter, chez certains entrepreneurs, l'espoir d'une fortune rapide. Au dernier Salon du Bour-get, on ne comptait pas moins de soixante types d'appareils proposés au public. Un peu de tout, et pas toujours du plus sérieux! Bon nombre de machines n'avaient jamais volé : les acheteurs seront les pilotes d'essai. Quelques autres modèles ont même été vendus sur plan : les clients avanceront la trésorerie . . .

« Planche à voile du ciel », « 2 CV ou motocyclette de l'air », les qualificatifs imagés appliqués à ces engins reposent sur des arguments trompeurs — facilité de pilotage et prix avantageux. Profitant d'une réglementation provisoirement « ultralégère », les commerçants et la clientèle des U.l.m. évoluent dans les nuages. L'atterrissage risque d'être rude . . .

Un U.l.m. de construction sérieuse coûte obligatoirement cher. Le compte est vite fait : le moteur revient à 12 000 F, de même que la voilure en Dacron. Il faut ajouter des tubes en aluminium, des câbles et des petites fournitures de qualité aviation. L'assemblage exige de 70 à 80 heures de main-d'œuvre très qualifiée. On produit alors un U.l.m. « pendulaire » inspiré du deltaplane — le plus simple — pour 35 000 à 40 000 Francs, prix public. Pour un « deux ou trois axes », qui ressemble déjà à un petit avion, cette somme atteindra 15 000 ou 20 000 Francs de plus.

Actuellement, les importateurs fournissent la majorité du parc. Cette année, ils ont vendu, début janvier, 60 *Quicksilver* américains et 92 *Pathfinder* anglais. Mais la tendance est à la construction sous licence.

De petits fabricants tentent tout de même de faire voler « 100% français ». Une belle aventure. Ainsi la société Aile est-elle exemplaire : elle est née de la rencontre d'un financier, d'un gestionnaire et d'un passionné, Patrick Lemonnier. Ce dernier, conseillé par des amis, ingénieurs chez Marcel Dassault, construisait son propre U.l.m. dans son jardin. . . . Soixante-cinq appareils « Patrilor » fabriqués par Aile volent aujourd'hui.

Une autre société française, Agriplane, a livré cette année 50 appareils pour le traitement — pulvérisation, épandage — des cultures. L'U.l.m.

est idéal pour les petites surfaces, l'avion, lui, n'étant rentable que sur 150 à 200 hectares d'un seul tenant.

On fabrique des U.l.m. un peu partout, et parfois un peu n'importe comment. Le Syndicat des constructeurs d'aéronefs ultralégers, qui vient de se créer, s'emploie à moraliser la profession et tente d'imposer des normes draconiennes de qualité. Pas facile, car les U.l.m. restent dispensés du « certificat de navigabilité » . . .

Le marché est prometteur. Selon des estimations sérieuses, un parc de 40 000 appareils pourrait être nécessaire dans les cinq prochaines années, compte tenu du renouvellement d'un matériel qui est, par nature, relativement fragile. Les « pendulaires », qui se vendent encore très bien, grâce à une clientèle venue du deltaplane, céderont progressivement du terrain devant les « deux ou trois axes », qui permettent, par leur pilotage, de passer à l'avion « en vrai ».

Les services de l'hélicoptère

Mis à part le vol stationnaire, l'U.l.m. peut rendre bien des services jusqu'ici réservés à l'hélicoptère : il décolle et atterrit n'importe où, vole à très faible altitude, en sécurité et à basse vitesse (40 km/h). Le prix de l'heure de vol est le huitième de celui de l'heure d'hélicoptère, et le prix d'achat, le dixième.

En outre, les pilotes professionnels, qui viennent de constituer un syndicat, ont bien l'intention de mettre un frein à la prolifération anarchique et dangereuse des écoles de pilotage d'U.l.m. Il en existe actuellement plus de 60. En l'absence de législation, n'importe qui, à condition de posséder un appareil et un bout de terrain, peut s'improviser moniteur. Les heures de vol sont vendues de 300 à 400 Francs. Et les « forfaits lâcher » en stage d'une semaine, de 2 000 à 4 000 Francs, sans brevet reconnu.

En 1982, on a comptabilisé huit accidents mortels en U.l.m. Et, dès le départ du tour de France, un équipage s'est blessé dans un atterrissage forcé.

L'espoir d'achats en grand nombre, par l'Armée ou par des administrations, fait rêver les constructeurs. Déjà, deux compagnies de troupes aéroportées expérimentent des U.l.m. Au Salon du Bourget, un *Baroudeur* arborait un missile et un lance-roquettes! La gendarmerie, les Eaux et forêts, les Douanes pourraient — à l'exemple des Coast Guards américains — trouver dans l'U.l.m. un moyen de transport simple et peu onéreux. Le rêve d'Icare au marché public!

Jacques Potherat
L'Express
July 22, 1983
747 words

Sample Interlingual Précis – Analysis of Content

The analysis can be jotted down in point form.

Paragraph 1 • ultralight aircraft are becoming increasingly popular in France

Paragraph 2 • ultralight sales are booming, even for aircraft still in design stage
• many different models are being put out by profit-minded businessmen

Paragraph 3 • popular misconception: that ultralight is easy to fly and cheap
• underregulation of field

Paragraph 4 • well-made ultralights are actually quite expensive (35,000 - 60,000 francs)

Paragraph 5 • most models are imported

Paragraph 6 • but there are some domestic French manufacturers e.g. Aile

Paragraph 7 • e.g. Agriplane, which makes ultralights for crop-dusting, etc.

Paragraph 8 • lack of legislation governing manufacturing
• manufacturers' association is trying to introduce strict quality control

Paragraph 9 • market is growing and looks promising
• movement towards more sophisticated models

Paragraph 10 • ultralight offers many of same services as the helicopter and is much less expensive

Paragraph 11 • lack of regulation of ultralight flying schools
• pilots' association seeks to remedy situation

Paragraph 12 • there have been deaths and injuries

Paragraph 13 • manufacturers are hoping to sell ultralights to government, the military, etc.

Sample Interlingual Précis – Major Themes

The ideas in the text can be grouped around the following major recurrent themes:

1. The ultralight's popularity
2. Manufacturers of the ultralight (foreign and domestic)
3. Misconceptions concerning the ultralight
4. Lack of regulation of the field (manufacturers and flying schools)
5. The growing market for the ultralight

Sample Interlingual Précis – The Final Version

The Age of Icarus

The ultralight aircraft is the latest fad in France these days. Many different models are being designed and manufactured by enterprising businessmen eager to ride the wave of the ultralight's popularity—some models are even being sold when they are still in the planning stage.

Most of the models on the market are British or American imports, but domestic manufacturing is growing. Two successful small French companies are Aile, which began with a home-made ultralight, and Agriplane, which manufactures ultralights for crop-dusting.

There are two common misconceptions about ultralights: that they are easy to fly, and that they are inexpensive. Actually, ultralights have been involved in several fatal crashes, and the price for a well-made model ranges from 35,000 to 60,000 francs.

One serious problem is the lack of legislation governing the ultralight industry: at present, ultralights need not be certified airworthy. However, a recently formed manufacturers' association is hoping to bring in stringent regulations to guarantee quality. Similarly, a pilots' association is trying to introduce regulations governing ultralight flying schools, which are not currently controlled by legislation.

The future market for ultralights, especially for the more sophisticated models, looks promising. The ultralight can perform many of the functions of the helicopter, and at a fraction of the cost. Moreover, manufacturers are hoping to expand their market by convincing the government to use ultralights for military and law-enforcement purposes. Soon the ultralight may be a common form of transportation.

249 words

Exercise 35 – Interlingual Précis-Writing

Write a précis of the following text *in English*. Your text should be approximately 50 words.

Vers la fin du IXe siècle de notre ère, l'Afrique romaine était à son apogée. Depuis plusieurs siècles le grenier de Rome, ses plaines et ses collines étaient parsemées de villas dont les riches propriétaires s'adonnaient aux plaisirs de la chasse, qui figurent si souvent sur les mosaïques qui font la gloire des musées nord-africains. L'Afrique s'enorgueillissait aussi de ses villes, dotées de monuments grandioses par les grands personnages, sénateurs et consuls, pour ne pas dire parfois des empereurs, qui vantaient leur succès en embellissant leur ville natale. La capitale de l'Afrique était Carthage, deuxième cité de l'Empire, « une ville bouillonnante d'activité, prompte à se passionner pour les plaisirs faciles du théâtre et de l'hippodrome, mais fière aussi de sa culture et curieuse des grands problèmes théologiques et philosophiques ». Elle était aussi connue pour ses mœurs légères : quand saint Augustin y entreprit ses études universitaires en 371, elle lui apparut comme « une chaudière des honteuses amours ».

C.M. Wells
"L'Afrique à la veille des invasions arabes"
University of Ottawa Quarterly
January-March 1982
156 words

Exercise 36 – Interlingual Précis-Writing

Write a précis *in English* of the following paragraph, reducing it to approximately 75 words.

Les postes de pêche sédentaire établis par les marchands de Québec au XVIIIe et XIXe siècles sous le régime français se retrouvaient donc sur tout le pourtour de la côte gaspésienne, en particulier au Mont-Louis, à Gaspé, à Pabos et à Grande-Rivière, pour ne citer que les plus importants. Ces entreprises reposaient alors sur une main-d'œuvre professionnelle ou semi-professionnelle. Certains pêcheurs n'ayant pas que la pêche comme moyen de subsistance possédaient aussi une terre dans le haut du fleuve, hors des limites des postes de pêche. D'autres, par contre, établis à Québec ou sur la côte de la péninsule, vivaient exclusivement de la pêche et se considéraient « pêcheurs de profession ». Dans un cas comme dans l'autre, ces hommes se trouvaient souvent à court d'argent quand arrivaient les préparatifs d'une campagne; parce que les prêteurs se faisaient rares en Nouvelle-France, presque tous se tournaient alors vers des pourvoyeurs, ni plus ni moins que des marchands-prêteurs, pour soutenir financièrement leur entreprise. Ils s'adressaient le plus souvent à des marchands locaux. Mais il arrivait aussi qu'ils approchaient des hommes d'affaires intéressés aux pêches d'une façon ou de l'autre : soit que ces fournisseurs possédassent un poste de pêche, soit qu'ils fissent le commerce du poisson. Ces marchands consentaient d'autant plus volontiers le crédit demandé que s'offrait pour eux l'occasion de s'assurer en contrepartie de bons approvisionnements en morue sèche.

Mario Mimeault
" La continuité de l'emprise des compagnies de pêche françaises et jersiaises sur les pêcheurs au XVIIIe siècle – Le cas de la compagnie Robin"
Histoire sociale/Social History
Vol. XVIII, No. 35, May 1985
220 words

(Note: Footnotes have been omitted for the purpose of this exercise.)

Exercise 37 – Interlingual Précis-Writing

Write a précis of the following passage *in English*. Your précis should be one-third the length of the original French text. Be sure that your summary accurately reflects the attitude of the original.

Oui, comment parler d'autre chose? Comment ne pas y penser? Un spectre hante le monde depuis 1945, c'est celui du nucléaire. Cette rupture fondamentale dans la longue aventure du progrès, on a, bien sûr, tout fait pour la nier, la refuser, la gommer. On a prétendu l'intégrer dans l'exaltante continuité de l'âge des lumières et de la foi en l'homme. En faire une machine comme une autre, aussi neutre qu'une autre, ni bonne ni mauvaise, en somme, et dont les vertus dépendaient, selon la formule, de l'usage qu'en feraient les hommes. D'abord, on a commencé — puisque la providence avait pris soin de placer la bombe atomique entre les mains des Occidentaux — à proclamer que, malgré ses ravages bien culpabilisants, l'énergie nucléaire servait le Bien. Ensuite, quand les superpuissances sont arrivées à se partager le pouvoir atomique, on a célébré cette voie, toujours providentielle, qui débouchait sur la coexistence pacifique par l'impénétrable détour de l'équilibre de la terreur. On a enfin achevé d'exorciser le démon en découvrant l'âge d'or promis par « l'atome civil ». Puisqu'il était civil, il devenait civilisé. On manquait de pétrole, de charbon, d'énergie? L'Uranium, inépuisable panacée, nouvelle pierre philosophale, procurerait dés-ormais à nos modernes alchimistes la puissance depuis toujours rêvée sur la nature . . .

Mieux encore : les hérauts et les experts de la troisième révolution industrielle ont bien consenti à nous avertir des dangers de deux sciences, l'informatique et la génétique, dont les stupéfiants progrès pouvaient se retourner contre l'homme si l'on n'y prenait garde. Tout était à redouter de cette capacité nouvelle que l'homme s'est donnée de surveiller son prochain et de programmer aussi bien son intelligence que son esprit de soumission. Mais le nucléaire, lui, restait inviolé, inviolable, moyen, au contraire, de fournir ce surcroît de puissance, cet appui, ce levier, qui nous permettait de transformer en promesses toutes les menaces qui s'amoncellent à l'horizon. Aujourd'hui encore, la plupart du temps, c'est presque le même discours que l'on entend. Plus embarrassé peut-être, plus défensif sans doute. Mais aucune brèche, ni même aucune lézarde ne fissure les murailles de la certitude — ou plutôt de la foi.

Jean Daniel
Le Nouvel Observateur
April 9, 1979
348 words

Popularization-Summaries

A popularization-summary is an easily understood abridged version of a fairly complex original text. Writing a popularization-summary involves a combination of skills: not only must you determine and communicate the major ideas in the original, but you must also adapt the style and level of diction to suit a general readership. The popularized version should be simply and clearly worded and easy to understand; it should be less technical and more transparent than the original. Some technical detail will of course be lost; after all, you are summarizing.

Whereas the original text is fairly specialized and is aimed at an audience that shares with the author a certain expertise in the field, the popularized version is designed for an average reader with no specialized background. The specialized text is written by an expert for an expert; the popularized text may deal with specialized subject matter, but it is written for the general public.

The writing of the popularization-summary is a real test of your comprehension of the original; your ability to express the essence of a specialized text in simple terms is proof of your understanding of the material.

Two samples of popularizations, along with the original texts, are given to illustrate the process. Study each one; then write popularized summaries yourself for the exercises that follow.

Sample Original Text #1

The finding of an inverse relation between socioeconomic status of parents and impaired mental health is particularly significant because it indicates that successively lower parental status carries for the child progressively greater likelihood of inadequate personality adjustment in adulthood. The finding that one's current socioeconomic status is even more closely related to one's mental health suggests that the effects of low socioeconomic status are probably cumulative in that the vulnerable personalities developed by some low-status children prevent their upward mobility and destine them to the further burdens and stresses that low socioeconomic status adults typically encounter in the United States. Moreover, lower-class persons tend toward socially disturbing psychotic adaptations that further complicate their adjustment to an already stressful environment, while higher-status persons tend to respond to stress with neurotic responses that are socially more adaptive. Thus, the cumulative effects of unfavorable childhood and adult experiences on the lower-class person may result in a higher degree of vulnerability not only to mental illness but also to the development of more serious psychiatric symptoms.

International Dictionary of the Social Sciences,
ed. David L. Sills,
Macmillan, p. 224

Sample Popularized Summary #1

The poorer a family is, the greater the chance that its children will suffer from mental illness as they grow up. Children in lower-income groups are caught in a vicious circle: the cumulative effects of poverty on their mental health prevent them from improving their lot as they become adults and thus from escaping a very stressful environment. People in higher income groups are able to adapt to stress in a more socially acceptable way, whereas those from the lower classes are more likely to develop serious psychiatric problems.

Sample Original Text #2

In a wave of articles published across North America, other journalists have joined John Kenneth Galbraith in an attack on monetarism. Their basic assertion is that monetarism has been tried and has failed.

I have been careful to use the word assert because close examination of the facts does not substantiate any such claim and, moreover, the evidence which is typically educed to support the claim is often totally unrelated to issues of monetarism.

Part of the difficulty with the castigation of monetarism and the excoriation of its principal advocate, Milton Friedman, is the fact that monetarism as a label has been used to describe a wide range of economic policies which more appropriately should be called conservatism.

Monetarism as a feature of public policy is a very specific prescription for the conduct of macro-economic stabilization. That is to say, the financial policies pursued by the central government.

The basic, reasonable message of monetarism is that if in the long term a country wishes to have a low rate of inflation, then its money supply should not be allowed to grow much faster than its ability to produce goods and services.

As a practical matter, very few professional economists disagree with the proposition that low rates of inflation are not attainable in the face of continuous excessive expansion of the money supply. So, on a purely technical level, monetarism is merely a description of what, in this imperfect world, is possible with regard to stable prices.

Michael Walker
The Financial Post
February 28, 1981, p. 18

Sample Popularized Summary #2

A group of journalists support J.K. Galbraith's claim that monetarism has failed. Yet their grounds for dismissing monetarism and its principal advocate, Milton Friedman, are unsubstantiated. These critics are in fact using the term "monetarism" too loosely: the economic policies they are referring to would more appropriately be called "conservatism".

Monetarism is a very specific type of financial policy used by the central government to reduce inflation by ensuring that the country's money supply does not outstrip its ability to produce goods and services. Most economists agree that inflation cannot be kept down if the money supply grows too quickly. Monetarism is simply a way of keeping prices stable.

Exercise 38 – Popularizing and Summarizing

Write a popularized summary of the following paragraph, in approximately 30 words.

Streams of sea water containing effluent from damaged animal tissues stimulated *Nassarius obsoletus*, *Nassarius reticulatus* and *Nassarius G. mutabilis* to move towards the source of the smell. However, the direction of movement was predominantly upstream only after some days of starvation. After 4 days of laboratory starvation, 13/80 *N. obsoletus* tested in a circular current containing crab extract moved upstream, compared with 7/40 in clean water . . . . After 2 weeks of starvation, the response to crab extract was distinct, 19/23 snails moving upstream compared with only 3/23 in clean sea water ($X^2 = 19.6$; $P < 0.001$).

Mary Crisp
"Effects of Feeding on the Behaviour of Nassarius Species (Gastropoda: Prosobranchia)"
Journal of Marine Biology
1978, No. 58.
93 words

Exercise 39 – Popularizing and Summarizing

Write a popularized summary of the following excerpt from a Canadian statute, in approximately 140 words. Your summary should convey the main ideas of the text in simple, non-specialized language.

3. No person shall manufacture for sale, sell, offer, expose or have in possession for sale any product that is a colourable imitation of a maple product unless such product or the container thereof is legibly marked with the manufacturer's name and address, the ingredients of such product and the words "artificially maple flavoured". R.S., c. 172, s. 3.

4. No person shall manufacture for sale, sell, offer, expose or have in possession for sale, or ship or cause to be shipped, any maple product that is adulterated. R.S., c. 172, s. 4.

5. Except as hereinbefore provided or in the trade name or description of artificial maple flavours or extracts, no person shall use the word "maple" alone or in combination with any word, letter or syllable on any label on other than a maple product. R.S., c. 172, s. 5.

6. The Minister (of Agriculture) or the Minister of Consumer and Corporate Affairs may designate any person as an inspector for the purposes of this Act. 1968-69, c. 28, s. 105.

7. Any inspector charged with the enforcement of this Act is empowered:
(a) to enter at will and inspect any or all buildings of whatever character in connection with any manufacturing or packing plant, sugar camp, or any hotel, restaurant, retail or wholesale store, warehouse, railway car, truck, boat or other conveyance where maple products or imitation maple products are being manufactured or offered for sale or being carried or held for carriage, and to take samples of any substance purporting to be a maple product or a colourable imitation thereof; any sample so taken may be paid for

at current prices and sealed in the presence of the producer, manufacturer, proprietor or carrier or his agent; the sample so taken and sealed shall be sent to the Department of Agriculture at Ottawa for analysis or investigation; the person from whom a sample is taken may require that a check sample be taken, sealed and left with him;

(b) to examine the books or records of manufacturing or packing plants;

(c) to seize in any place mentioned in paragraph (a) and seal for analysis, inspection or investigation any article that he believes to be an adulterated maple product or intended for adulteration of any maple product or any maple product that is not graded, packed, marked, labelled, produced or held in premises in compliance with this Act or the regulations and to dispose of any product or substance so seized as the Minister (of Agriculture) may direct. R.S., c. 172, s. 7.

Maple Products Industry Act
Revised Statutes of Canada—1970
Vol. V, Chapter M-2
417 words

Abstracting

Abstracting is a specialized form of summarizing, and is usually done by the author of the document himself, by a specialist in the subject matter, or by a specialist in the art of abstracting. Courses in abstracting are sometimes given as part of information-science and library-science programs. Abstracting can also be included in writing skills programs, within the context of a course in technical writing or advanced writing techniques.

Standard rules and conventions for abstracting can be found in the American National Standards Institute's *American National Standard for Writing Abstracts*.[1] "House" rules and conventions are often provided by individual abstracting services. The following suggestions are based largely on the excellent advice that can be found in Edward T. Cremmins' *The Art of Abstracting*.[2]

Cremmins explains that the indicative abstract describes the purpose, scope, and methods found in the original, whereas the informative abstract describes the purpose, scope, methods, results, conclusions, and recommendations. He suggests a three-stage approach to abstracting: he breaks the process down into what he calls "retrieval reading," "creative reading," and "critical reading." The first step (retrieval reading) is to read the text analytically, identifying the nature of each section of the text and indicating the themes by using a system of marginalia. The second step (creative reading) involves grouping all the relevant material into general categories—for example, bringing together all the information on purpose, scope, and method under one heading—then rereading the information in each category, and summarizing it in one or several concise sentences. In the third step, the material assembled and drafted in step two is edited and revised; the abstractor endeavours to polish the text, making sure that the sentences flow together and that there is no unnecessary repetition.

For additional background on abstracting, see the relevant section of Chapter 1, Part One.

Writing an Informative Abstract: Dos and Don'ts

Do

- Read the text analytically, with the purpose of identifying information to be included in the abstract.
- Include the *purpose* of the work done, the *methodology* used, the *results* obtained, and the *conclusions* reached.
- Be as informative as possible.
- Use full, connected sentences and standard English; follow conventional rules governing grammar and punctuation.
- Avoid overuse of the passive.
- Use the third person.
- Use standard nomenclature.
- Make sure that your abstract is no more than 250 words in length (if the original is of standard length).

Do not

- Include your critical assessment of the document.
- Change the meaning of the original document.
- Include background information or information concerning work done by others, unless the document studies or evaluates this work in depth.
- Include any information not in the original.
- Use jargon, circumlocutions, or unnecessary words.
- Repeat yourself.
- Go into excessive detail.

A Sample Abstract

You can find a wide variety of samples in abstracting journals in the reference room of your local library. Abstracting and indexing journals are used extensively to locate articles in almost all specialized fields.

A typical abstract is given below; study the type of information presented and the format used. This particular abstract is taken from a 1986 issue of the journal *Language and Language Behavior Abstracts*, and describes the content of an article on child language acquisition, entitled "Children's Sensitivity to Comprehension Failure in Interpreting a Nonliteral Use of an Utterance," by Brian Ackerman.

> The relative sensitivity of children and adults to both their own and another listener's failure to understand literal and non-literal uses of utterances is studied. Three separate experiments, each involving 3 age groups (7 years, 10 years, and adult) were conducted. [The subjects'] interpretations of stories containing either a literal or a nonliteral utterance and responses to those stories provided by other listeners were assessed. The results showed that, while the 7-year-olds did not evaluate the listener's understanding effectively, both groups of children understood well the speaker's nonliteral intent and were quite sensitive to instances of their own lack of comprehension. It is speculated that the difficulties encountered by the younger children may have stemmed from their failure to use their own interpretations of the speaker's intent as an evaluative standard.

1. *American National Standard for Writing Abstracts* (New York: American National Standards Institute, Inc., 1979).
2. Edward T. Cremmins, *The Art of Abstracting* (Philadelphia: ISI Press, 1982).

Exercise 40 — Abstracting

Write an abstract of 100-130 words for the following article.

Contemporary Ethical Issues Surrounding Electroconvulsive Therapy

The use of electroconvulsive therapy (ECT) highlights the conflict between scientific psychiatry and modern society. Despite the great advances that psychiatry has accomplished in the past 30 years, especially in the treatment of the affective disorders and schizophrenia, this new psychiatry with a scientific base has been criticized and caricatured as too biological and impersonal, and too tied to the medical model and to authoritarian patterns of practice. The biological therapies create new ethical dilemmas because of their ability to profoundly influence thinking, feeling and behavior. On the other hand, psychiatry as a science has been criticized as inexact with too few correlations with objective and verifiable data. To most medical practitioners, ECT is an empirically proven treatment that can be used against certain psychiatric syndromes of unknown etiology that are, nevertheless, associated with a high risk of morbidity and mortality. To a vocal minority, both professional and public, the use of ECT is an affront to the values of a free and democratic society.

Modern society is characterized by rapid social changes and global communications. People have grouped together to challenge the power of 'the establishment', governments, institutions and professions. Individuals and groups have demanded autonomy and freedom from unnecessary government and institutional interference and intrusions. As never before, the ethical principles of those in high office, and of governments and professions, are being examined and influenced by the public (look at Vietnam, Watergate or the Peace initiative). In the health care field, modern societies are demanding public accountability for the rationalization of health services, universal accessibility to treatment, quality control, cost effectiveness, clarification of the rights of patients, and the setting of ethical standards in biomedical research and education.

The difference between the attitudes of the general public or lawyers and the medical profession is largely explained by different value systems rather than by scientific evaluation. Even within psychiatry there is not complete agreement and there are a variety of ethical principles that a psychiatrist can follow when he/she prescribes or does not prescribe ECT. The two main opposing ethical frameworks will be described— paternalistic and libertarian (or Kantian). A third framework that I call "applied clinical ethics" will also be outlined and its advantages highlighted.

Paternalism has been a characteristic of healer-patient interactions for thousands of years. Supporters of the need for paternalism argue that the suffering and distress of the patient, and the knowledge, experience and skills of a physician, prevent the formation of an objective rational contractual relationship. Patients with "dis-ease" want comfort and hope, more than information or the need to make uninformed decisions, which can too easily interfere with comfort and increase pain and anxiety. In psychiatry, many psychotic patients have been given ECT against their will because the psychiatrist acted in the patient's best interests, believing that the patient would likely be substantially improved with ECT, but that he would languish indefinitely in a psychosis without it. In this type of relationship the patient is usually dependent, passive, uninformed and powerless. However, the boundary between paternalism on the patient's behalf, and the (ab)use of power or inflexibility on the part of the physician is frequently blurred.

Paternalistic attitudes by professions and governments are less acceptable in our society as the population becomes more informed, more educated, less trustful, more active, assertive and desirous of power and responsibility in making treatment decisions.

Libertarian or Kantian ethics question the right or power of a person to make decisions for another. Rights of equality, autonomy and inviolability when applied to the citizen who becomes a patient, lead to the principles of free informed consent, the right to refuse treatment, and negotiated therapeutic contracts between physician and patient.

J.S. Mill stated this view clearly last century. "The only purpose for which power can be rightfully exercised over any member of a civilized community, against his will, is to prevent harm to others. His own good, either physical or moral, is not sufficient warrant". It is argued that we cannot protect a person from his own stupidity, silliness, foolishness or imprudence, even if it results in death or injury. Not only is this the stand taken by Szasz toward all psychiatric patients, but also it is the stand society takes toward the physically ill who refuse treatment for irrational reasons or toward alcoholics, drug addicts, habitual gamblers and others who are slowly destroying themselves.

Politically educated people have little tolerance for oligarchic government rule (as in South Africa) and by extension want more equality and democracy and less paternalism from both politicians and professionals. Civil libertarians, and psychiatrists who look objectively at our own profession, can find many skeletons in our psychiatric house and recognize the need for some decrease in the use of paternalism—for example, the use of regressive depatterning ECT, the 30-year delay in the routine use of general anaesthesia with ECT, or the continued routine use of bilateral ECT in some settings, are evidence that our profession does not police itself well. The literature abounds with examples of useless or harmful treatments including dunking and blood letting.

Following the Kantian code of ethics, as in the American Constitution, or the Canadian Charter of Rights and Freedoms, society will place very high priority on maintaining freedom and accepting individual deviance. To fight paternalism or other forms of social control, society will tighten up the rules on free informed consent, insisting on the patient's choice after complete disclosure of the advantages and disadvantages of recommended and alternative treatments. A patient's personal choice of reasonable treatments will override the physician's choice based on expediency, cost-benefit or efficiency. Patient advocates and surrogate decisions made by a court will replace decisions made by a treating physician or next of kin. A Kantian ethical stand would allow for involuntary hospitalization (to protect others) but not for involuntary treatment.

In the extreme, the application of this system of ethics presents a problem. Some individuals will be harmed because treatment is not given; the society can be held partly to blame, and loses part of its own humanity. The deontological principles of freedom and autonomy are unchanged because no room is made for cybernetic corrective feedback from clinical or social science or family members.

However, no society can ignore those who are unable to care for themselves. What is needed is a code of ethics that also includes an understanding of emotions—compassion, caring, respect for the individual, and appreciating a patient's need to be cared for. True justice requires an understanding beyond the intellectual. John Stuart Mill lived before Freud discovered the importance of emotions in our everyday lives. Mill developed and expanded a highly intellectual ethical argument for equality and individual freedom but it seems he regretted his own poor understanding of emotions and felt as if he had missed out on half of life.

I envision applied clinical ethics as a set of ethical rules that govern interactions between physician and patient in the context of a free and democratic society. Most patients are autonomous, in terms of being free and responsible, and Kantian principles will prevail. Some people are not autonomous because of immaturity or disease. However, we must recognize the importance of affective components in the development of motivation and values and acknowledge or document how emotions can interfere with autonomy. The only acceptable ethical goal of psychiatric intervention should be to maintain or re-establish patient autonomy or freedom. If autonomy cannot be re-established then intervention cannot be justified.

On the other hand, we must also recognize the high value that our society places on freedom and autonomy. Society has a right to protect this. Our society will expect the government to be accountable to the public, and oversee the ethical practices of a profession. Court reviews and appeals, the acceptance of a patient's choice of a less intrusive treatment, and the close examination of professional treatment decisions, are likely to be the minimal requirements that our society will demand in order to feel reassured that psychiatry will not be misused as it has in other times and in other places.

Since our society places such a high value on freedom and autonomy, it is likely that the vast majority of our patients value this as well. To ignore the value they place on freedom by resorting to paternalistic behavior is to dehumanize them and risk damage to their self-esteem. We no longer take away patient's belongings because we recognize that this can have a deep and long lasting effect on self-esteem; the same is true of civil and legal rights. Society has a right to protect itself. Individuals have a right to their day in court in order to maintain self-esteem at some level and thus fight the dependency, passivity and ignorance which is an inevitable by-product of paternalism. Clinical studies will have to address the meaning of autonomy and the definition of a lack of autonomy. In addition, patients who are recipients of paternalistic approaches to treatment will be compared to patients who have an opportunity to exert their civil rights to see if there are differences in self-esteem. Studies such as these could influence ethical belief systems and help society to find the correct balance of competing values.

B.F. Hoffman, M.D.
Psychiatric Journal of the University of Ottawa
Vol. XI, No. 2, June-July 1986
1,522 words

(Note: Footnotes have been omitted for the purpose of this exercise.)